THE COVID-19 MUSICAL

I DON'T BEG PARDON

(I'm Talking B*ll*cks from the Rose Garden)

MIKE CASHMAN

with PETER, FRED & HILARY CASHMAN, PETER COOK, and PAUL SHRIMPTON

Published by Viewdelta Press
Paperback ISBN 978-1916248649
January 2021

Viewdelta IDBP202101150115
Produced in United Kingdom

Dedication

This book is dedicated to all those who have inspired us and to the very talented original writers whose lyrics we have discarded with thanks (with occasional exceptions – for example, one verse of "The Sentry Song" by W.S. Gilbert which we couldn't bear to delete from "Things that Will Astonish You"). It is dedicated also to their musical friends, whose tunes are in our heads as we write, and in some cases now on our CD with our irreverent words.

I like to think that the modifications would have had the full approval of Gilbert & Sullivan and of Flanders & Swann. Maybe Shakespeare too?

What, Yet More Parody Songs?

I had only planned to write two satire books.

But I had reckoned without the UK Government's ability to take the need to "Laugh Rather than Cry" to a new level. We genuinely live in a country where our Prime Minister's early response to the threat of coronavirus was to talk of going into a phone box and emerging as Superman (Greenwich, February 3rd). We live with the consequences of that attitude. And so, there were more aspects that were begging to be lampooned.

I had written "Misuse of power, misleading the electorate and political inconsistency are fruitful triggers for satire - a song declaring that the Government had fulfilled all its duties, following due process, is unlikely to raise a chuckle. Let's just say that this was a particularly fruitful period for these satirical songs". This continued to be true.

When Roland White of The Sunday Times asked if I was writing "Coronavirus the Musical", my first reaction was that such a title might be considered in poor taste. But I think I agree with John Cleese that although there can be a danger of offending, exploring that edge can sometimes yield the deepest humour.

Please understand that those bereaved from Covid-19 and other causes in 2020 are close to my heart, and in various ways I have sought to support. That support now includes a commitment that 100% of any profits from the sale of Viewdelta Press books and CDs will be sent to coronavirus charities. The existence and scale of such profits depends on you, the customer. Initially the chosen charity will be the Disasters Emergency Committee; I have worked on DEC projects in Kenya, Ethiopia, Nepal and Sierra Leone (Ebola) and from personal experience I have a high regard for the rigour and effectiveness that is established for DEC projects.

But on reflection, the theme of a Musical provided some useful structure for the reader. This Musical is not one story with a consistent set of characters as in "Brexit's a Musical Trick"; but as we prepared the CD of 21 recorded songs the structure of a five-Act musical provided a way to organise this eclectic mix.

There is far more content in the book than we could fit onto a single CD – but we hope that you will buy the CD (or USB) as well, for maximum enjoyment of what we have prepared for you. The songs were recorded at the homes of, for example, Leon Berger and of Selwyn Tillett (Leon and Selwyn perform all the Flanders & Swann and Gilbert & Sullivan songs), of Zena Wigram who sings in most of the Act 4 ("Distraction") songs, and in my own home during a week in August, where Ben Chambers of Sixteen Million Rising recorded in a socially distanced manner, one singer at a time, and mixed the results afterwards to produce the album that you can now buy.

Those who are looking for a politically neutral commentary should look elsewhere. The songs in this book do not take a kindly view of those who seek to mislead, and that leads us to be more critical of those who mislead more. But if you want further justification of the lyrics or titles, try checking www.viewdelta.blogspot.com, and search for the relevant subject, such as "Durham". There are a couple of entries directly relevant in support of the appropriateness of our book title.

As I complete the initial edition, we face floods and challenges on all fronts, with a new variant of the virus, and business which was given barely a week to implement what politicians took 235 weeks to dream up, once the Deal was known. But in the midst of all this, I hope that this book informs and amuses you, and that you can write a review and/or recommend online, which will help to bring the enjoyment of this book to a wider audience.

Mike Cashman January 2021

Guide to Contents

Our focus is all of the political and Public Health events of 2020, and the B-word is not therefore absent from this work, though it is not the main focus. I have brought forward just one song from the earlier Musical, "Failure Doesn't Matter in the Past", Why? Well, it sets the scene and context for much of what follows – a Government with its mind elsewhere, and with priorities other than Public Health.

There are some "Before" songs ("Gestation") and "After the Musical" songs (Act 999), and also a couple of interludes – Shakespeare in Lockdown and some excuses in short verse for absence from work. On the CD the Lockdown Shakespeare playlets form interludes between the Acts, but we have grouped them together in the book.

The original lyrics (for each song that has been imitated) and recordings of it should be available online. For most songs the words here should match the tune exactly, so you should be able to karaoke them if you would like to. Occasionally there is an extra verse or two compared to the original.

Any dates shown are the dates on which I wrote the pieces concerned – sometimes a few days after the news story. But the songs are arranged thematically rather than in strict chronological order. You can find an individual song using an index at the back, either by the new title or by the original title of the imitated work.

As with the earlier books, this work is intended to inform as well as amuse. More on the earlier books in the pages at the end.

You'll see from the front cover that there are quite a number of contributors. It was a great pleasure to sing an impromptu duet with Peter Cook when we were at the European Commission in London in January 31st. Some of the contributors share my surname. I didn't make them write these songs, they just wanted to do it.

Well, that's how this all started. We hope you enjoy the result

Contents

Gestation

We faced a worldwide pandemic with a Prime Minister who disliked full briefs, and skipped meetings of the COBRA emergency strategy group.
So, let us deal first with the pre-occupations of January and February which were mostly nothing to do with coronavirus.

Boris Jones' Diary

Have you got Big Pants

Yes but they keep catching fire?

What will you do about that?

I have asked the team to send me Shorter Briefs

CLARIFICATION: The Short Briefs should have a backside and a front side, and that's all

No Long Briefs

22 February 2020

As through all his papers he leafs
Hearing of Britain's new griefs,
We're told that we ought to
Make everything shorter
As Boris can't cope with Long Briefs.

Boris Has Got a Little List

Inspired by*: "I've got a Little List" – The Mikado, Gilbert & Sullivan "*

Not surprisingly this seems to be of the most often adapted songs, so I thought it was time for a Boris Johnson version - particularly since we know he does indeed have a little list, or maybe a big list.

December 2019, edited June 2020

1. As some days it may happen
That a victim must be found,
I've got a little list.
I've got a little list.

Of interfering bodies where
I do not like their sound.
They never would be missed.
They never would be missed.

There's doomsters, gloomsters, with computers,
Think it's cut and dried.
And people who are backward-looking,
Asking why I lied.
The people who remind me
That I said this Deal's wrong,

And poets like Mike Cashman
Who put all my words in song.

There's pedants on the Irish Sea
Whose fears I have dismissed.
They never would be missed.
They never would be missed.

Chorus: He's got 'em on the list.
He's got 'em on the list.
And they'd none of them be missed.
They'd none of them be missed.

2. The Appellant who attacks my plans,
Just like a girly swot.
The interventionist;
I've got her on the list.

The Judges in Supreme Court tell me
So much legal rot.
They never would be missed.
They never would be missed

And judges independent
Who may well go down the pub,
Which means I cannot nobble them

While at the Garrick Club.
Then critics who spot my mistakes
And make a lot of fuss.
And people who take me to court
For lying on a bus.

Judicial Re-view by the Courts
Who think our arms they'll twist;
That never would be missed.
That never would be missed.

Chorus: He's got 'em on the list.
He's got 'em on the list.
And they'd none of them be missed.
They'd none of them be missed

3. There's independent fact checkers
Detecting all the lies.
The nosy journalist!
I've got him on the list.

And investigators interviewing
Like some Private Eyes.
They never would be missed.
They never would be missed

And while we're on the subject,
Those satirical cartoons,
In papers that are edited
By left wing crazy loons,
The neighbours who record my rows.
The folk with some old quote,
Yes, people who remember all
The stupid things I wrote.

And anyone who thinks they can
The Tory rule resist;
I don't think they'd be missed.
I'm sure they'd not be missed.

Chorus: He's got 'em on the list.
He's got 'em on the list.
And they'd none of them be missed.
They'd none of them be missed.

4. The Chancellor that had advisers
Who he would not sack,
He was obstructionist!
I put him on the list.

And Permanent-ish Secret'ries
I feel I can attack

They never would be missed.
They never would be missed.

Protections for child refugees -
Lord Dubs who quotes their plights
And regulations mandat'ry
That dream up workers' rights,
Like pettifogging standards that
Say folk must have time off,
Which limit all the profits
For the Tory owner toff,

Climate-change reductions from
Th' environmentalist.
They never would be missed.
They never would be missed.

Chorus: He's got 'em on the list.
He's got 'em on the list.
And they'd none of them be missed.
They'd none of them be missed.

5. All interviewers from the Press
Who nasty questions ask.
The interruptionist;
I've got her on the list.

The BBC when hounding me
Who're taking me to task.
They never would be missed.
They never would be missed.

And Channel 4 who wouldn't have
As stand-in Gove or Dad.
There's petty-spot examiners who
Scrutinise each ad.
And nationalist candidates
Not fit to hold our coats,
Who stand in our elections
Just to steal the Tory votes.

And then the Labour Party
Who are simply Bolshevist .
I don't think they'd be missed.
I'm sure they'd not be missed.

> Chorus: You may put 'em on the list.
> You may put 'em on the list.
> And they'd none of them be missed.
> They'd none of them be missed.

Big Ben's non-bonging

There was concern among Brexiteers including the Prime Minister was to whether Big Ben could "bong" as the UK left the EU.

15 January 2020

If for decades you all had been thronging
With folk who for Brexit were longing,
Then do not have you
Something better to do
Than carping on Big Ben's non-bonging?

"Something better to do" could be planning for the UK coronavirus response

Propaganda

Boris Johnson creates new film factory to help with propaganda efforts.

To judge by his new memoranda
He doesn't like objective candour;
So to spin some more mystery
He's rewriting history
With Brexit film team propaganda.

You'll believe that a Boris can lie

Boris Johnson was pictured, arms out in flying mode, with Prince Harry.
Shortly afterwards at Greenwich he revealed his "Superman" fantasy.

About Harry you may wonder why
To stay here he'll no longer try
To cope with Press stricture;
Examine this picture
You'll believe that a Boris can lie.

This scary pandemic

I cannot tell a lie; although I aired this view privately in January 2020, I did not write the limerick until later.

It's not just a point academic
Or some unprovoked new polemic;
The deaths now projected.
One per cent of infected?
We should take note of this scary pandemic.

Little Yellow Mini

Inspired by "Big Yellow Taxi"

Also inspired by co-author Peter Cook's return in a little yellow Brexit mini from Brussels to the European Commission office in London – where we were saying "Goodbye and Thank You"

31 January 2020

They made load of lies
And they said that Brexit's done
With a protocol for Ireland
And plans to achieve it? None.

Don't it always seem to go
That you don't know what you've got till its gone?
They made load of lies
And they said that Brexit's done.

So the little yellow mini
Went to Brussels. Carpe Diem.
Came back to join us
So the London EC would see'em.

Don't it always seem to go,
That you don't know what you've got
Till it's gone?
They made load of lies
And they said that Brexit's done,

Hey fisher fisher
Who thought you'd rule the seas?

Your fish go to Europe
And there's conditions for Deals.
Please!

Don't it always seem to go
That you don't know what you've got
Till it's gone?
They made load of lies.
And they said that Brexit's done.

Late last night
I heard him saw "It's dawn".
And the yellow blue flag
From its place was torn.
Don't it always seem to go
That you don't know what you've got
Till it's gone?
They made load of lies
And they said that Brexit's done.

Don't it always seem to go
That you don't know what you got
Till it's gone?
They made load of lies
And they said that Brexit's done.
How come?

They made load of lies
And they said that Brexit's done.
Hey hey hey
Made load of lies
And they said that Brexit's done.

Failure doesn't matter in the past

Inspired by "Beggar at the Feast"

Because it is very relevant to coronavirus, here is one song brought froward from "Brexit's a Musical Trick", which features two fictional characters, Cunnings and Boris ValBoris.
The song is inspired by the Boris Johnson "Superman" speech at Greenwich on 3rd February 2020 in which he predicted that coronavirus would work out well for the UK (i.e. for him) which would not shut down while other countries were over-cautious and shut down. He saw coronavirus as a positive event which would yield competitive advantage for Brexit Britain. He referred to entering a phone box as Clark Kent and emerging as "Superman". Those who wish to understand his declared preference for herd immunity and the late lockdown which cost thousands of lives would do well to watch this whole speech.

CUNNINGS
Ain't it a laugh?
Now how d'you feel
Forget what I said
On having a Deal.
Ireland command
Won't be obeyed.
And so we can't
Fix that East to West trade.

VALBORIS
Virus coming close,
Countries shutting down.
But here's me in the phone box
As the Clark Kent clown

CUNNINGS
Master of the Con.
Teller of the Lie.
Yesterday is soon gone
When you blink your eye.

VALBORIS
Never mind the facts.
Give me your support.
Optimism to the max,

CUNNINGS
Indeed you ought.

VALBORIS
Trading we will need a system.
Should have thought of that before.

CUNNINGS
But we took our pledges.
We took them and we pissed them up the wall.

VALBORIS
Others will shut down,
That is not for us.
Superman is flying
To his big red bus.
Herd immunity,
Mostly old will die.
Meanwhile we'll pretend to Build.
I don't know why.

CUNNINGS & VALBORIS
Somehow we'll be like Australia.
Check how well that tale will last.
Just another word for failure;
Failure doesn't matter in the past.

Passports Blue

Inspired by: "Somewhere. Over The Rainbow" .

22 February 2020

Some way, after our exit, Passports Blue.
That is why we did Brexit;
Passports are blue for you.

Some day, after this hit-show,
And each lie,
Try to work out the shit-show;
Yes, I think you'll ask why.

Some day we buggered up our trade,
While Boris and his rich chums played,
With fire.
Their bases now abroad are found.
They made big bets against the pound,
Helped by the Liar.

Some day, though made abroad now, Passports Blue.
Leavers want to applaud now.
I don't know why they do.

Travel, all over Europe, we could go.
Now, check, each time a visa?
What a disastrous show.
If with blue passports we can't go
To all those places that we know
Why, please, why can't we go?

A Fridge! A Fridge! My Brexit For a Fridge !

Another part of the field.

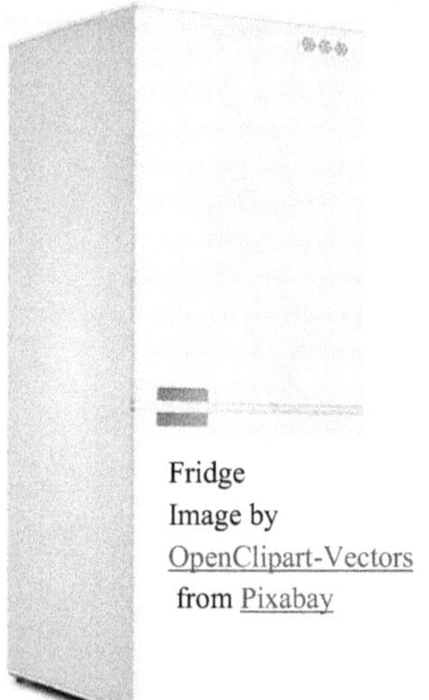

Fridge
Image by OpenClipart-Vectors from Pixabay

Enter KING BORIS the LAST, in the background, and CUNNINGS.

Alarums: excursions

Enter SABISKI

Tweets and blogs horrible.

Social media storm.

SABISKI is wounded by his own poisoned pen.

The KING is loyal to SABISKI, and stays with him.

SABISKI cries out against those who have used his poisoned pen against him.

He dies, supported by KING BORIS.

Enter FACT-CHECKERS and forces fighting;

to them, CUNNINGS

CUNNINGS

Rescue, my Lord of Johnson must not suffer!

PM enacts more porkies than a man,

Daring an opposite to all things rougher.
His fridge is gone, and by the lake he stands
Sneering at Corbyn, fight we that old duffer.
But save PM, or else we're down the pan!
Alarums and tweets

KING BORIS THE LAST
A fridge! a fridge! my Brexit for a fridge!

CUNNINGS
Withdraw, my lord; I'll help you to a fridge.

KING BORIS THE LAST
Slave, I have set my life upon a lie,
And I will stand the hazard of the die:
I think there be six fact checks in the field;
Five have I hid to-day yet more's reveal'd.
A fridge! a fridge! my Brexit for a fridge!

(A Special Adviser named Sabiski resigned after some of his unconventional opinions became public).

Act 1: Preparation (or not)

Prime Minister of all UK

Inspired by: Now he is the Ruler of the Queen's Navy (HMS Pinafore, Gilbert & Sullivan).
See also notes above on "Failure Doesn't Matter in the Past"

When I was a hack, I raised a laugh
With silly pieces for the Telegraph
Of bent bananas – what would get a rise
I wrote those articles though they were lies
(He wrote those articles though they were lies)
I wrote those articles and earned good pay
And now I am Prime Minister of all UK
(He wrote those articles and earned good pay
And now he is Prime Minister of all UK)

As journalist I cut a dash
And they made me the Mayor of the London Bash
I invented buses with a funny quirk
With a bridge and water cannons that didn't work
(With a bridge and water cannons that didn't work).
For the bridge and water cannons folk had to pay
But now I am Prime Minister of all UK
(For the bridge and water cannons folk had to pay

But now he is Prime Minister of all UK).

For the Leave campaign I rode a bus
With a slogan on the side that we won't discuss.
Well I hoped to lose in a glorious way
But sadly I won at the end of the day.
(But sadly he won at the end of the day)
I won that vote, though Theresa May
Was then Prime Minister of all UK
(He won that vote, though Theresa May
Was then Prime Minister of all UK).

But Theresa found that the Deal she wrote
Wouldn't get support in a Commons vote,
When we got her out then the vacancy
Was actually tailor-made for me,
(Was actually tailor-made you see).
They elected me in the Tory way
To be Prime Minister of all UK.
(They elected him in the Tory way
To be Prime Minister of all UK.)

"Oven Ready Deal" was my famous quote
That should be enough so I'd win the vote.
Well I said my deal is the only one.
Got MPs dismissed, got election done.

(Got MPs dismissed, got election done).
Got election done, then I'd have my say
And no-one else, I'm PM UK
(Got election done, then he'll have his say
And no-one else, he's PM UK).

Got my Deal passed, it did not take long.
But we had to discuss if Big Ben could Bong.
There's a virus coming which could be my chance,
If we don't lock down, let our trade enhance .
(If we don't lock down, let our trade enhance).
Let our trade enhance in that clever way.
I'm the Superman Prime Minister of all UK.
(Let the trade enhance in that clever way
He's the Superman Prime Minister of all UK).

When Shall We Three Tweet Again?

Inspired by: *"When Shall We Three Meet Again?"* .

8 March 2020

When shall we three tweet again?
Our funders like "No Deal" - that's plain.
When the Civil Servant walks.
When we've sabotaged the talks.
They'll be buggered up, no fear
Get 'em wrecked by June this year.
We're Patel and Gove and Truss -
Parked our broomsticks on the bus.
You've not seen the last of us
Where's the place where all you meant
To tell the lies? That's parliament!
And there to silence argument
We will all befoul the air
Fair is foul, and foul is fair,

Double, double, Brexit muddle;
Boats are burned, and we've made trouble.

Mix it in this Brexit Bowl;
Mandate of a dodgy poll.
Not so cute with face of frog.
Pull the wool, and spread the fog.
We're Patel and Truss and Gove -

Put the cauldron on the stove.
Dead Cats hiding Irish Seas;
Priti soon, their throat she'll squeeze.
If embarrassed when that's done, he'll
Talk of bridge or talk of tunnel.
Billions wasted in the muddle
Brexit heads for No Deal trouble.

Double, double, Brexit muddle;
Boats are burned, UK's in trouble.

Put the cauldron on the stove;
We're Patel and Truss and Gove.

Coronavirus comes to town.
Parliament can be shut down.
Of the raving Cummings elf
SPADS beware, you're on the shelf.
Scale of problem, what to do?
Haven't got a firkin clue.
With the raving Cummings elf
PJ masks to save our health?
Add thereto a lengthy brief.
Tires out Johnson - there's relief .

Double, double, Brexit muddle;
We've ensured UK's in trouble.

We know you've had enough of us
We're Patel and Gove and Truss.

So they say that she's a bully?
Let's investigate so fully.
Then we'll check the whole report,
See if he said what he ought.
But if people expect action,
We'll be busy with redaction.
If you're waiting for the hearings,
Think on Russian interference.
We're so charming in this muddle.
Brexit heads for No Deal trouble.

Double, double, Brexit muddle;
Funders gain from UK trouble.

We can evil things foretell;
Hear more from Gove, Truss, Patel.

EDITORIAL NOTE.

This poem is of course a work of fiction.

We do not wish to imply that:

- All members of the Government are openly advocating No Deal Brexit
- The reason for Tories being in favour of No Deal is related to the Tory Party Funders' alleged wish to profit from economic disaster
- Patel, Gove and Truss are all witches
- Any of them would say "firkin"
- They parked their broomsticks on the bus
- Priti Patel forced her senior Civil Servant out
- The report on Priti Patel's alleged bullying will be redacted or suppressed
- Mr Johnson has any difficulty with Long Briefs
- Mt Cummings' references to "PJ masks" had anything to do with coronavirus
- The mentions of bridge or tunnel for the Irish Sea were intended to distract from the Government's embarrassment about the Irish Sea.
-

So, just to clarify again, we do not wish to imply any of the above. We hope that clears up any confusion.

Why Why Why, Corona?

I wrote this as an encouragement to the behaviours we needed, with some inspiration from the four golden rules of the Bishop of St Alban's, and I made sure that the song was passed on to him.

It was used to promote a fund-raiser for community coronavirus support.

17 March 2020

Inspired by: "Delilah".

We saw this might be a fright
When it spread through our city,
We saw the bickering buying of bog roll –unkind;
That was so crazy,
Get what you need for today,
Don't go out of your mind.
Why Why Why Corona? (Yes we wanna wave) ,
Bye bye bye Corona.
Let me say,
That we have to all change our ways,
But keeping apart's
What we really must do now today.

Look where you live and to who
You can give some kind favour.
There may be someone right now
Who has needs, be aware.

Don't blooming panic.
No hoarding food
'Cos there's plenty for all if we share.
Why Why Why Corona? (Yes we wanna wave) ,
Bye bye bye Corona.
Let me say,
That we have to all change our ways,
But keeping apart's
What we really must do now today.

(Instrumental)
I stand here washing.
God save the Queen, front and back,
Till your hands are all clean
But keeping apart's
What we all have to do now today.

It's PPE, we need you see

Inspired by*: "Amarillo".*

23 April 2020

Choo choo choo choo choo choo choo choo
Choo choo choo choo choo choo choo choo
Choo choo choo choo choo choo choo choo
With the virus spreading,
And from us it's outward it's heading.
Now we've got to stay home.
There are limits on where we can now roam.
Every lonely moment, where we fear the bugs,
Leaves us isolated, not so many hugs.

Is this the way, Coronavirus?
Rishie Sunak says they won't fire us.
Just because Corinavirus
Months 1 2 3, please furlough me.
What did you say, coronavirus?
Why did that make bog roll buyers?
In the workplace, so few hire us.
Months 1 2 3, please furlough me.
Choo choo choo choo choo choo choo choo.
Choo choo choo choo choo choo choo choo.
Choo choo choo choo choo choo choo choo.
What strategy, to exit free?

There are ventilators,
And the EU still do not hate us.
Where's the PPE there?
How I'm longing to see PPE there.
In Select Committee.
There's an answer true.
And a later letter.
That said that answer's through.

Is this the way, Coronavirus
Do you make ministers liars?
Like before they caught the virus
It's PPE, we need you see

Is this the way, Coronavirus?
Have you invaded all inside us?
For a breakthrough we're desirous
But PPE we need you see

Choo choo choo choo choo choo choo choo
Choo choo choo choo choo choo choo choo
Choo choo choo choo choo choo choo choo
It's PPE we need you see

Choo choo choo choo choo choo choo choo
Choo choo choo choo choo choo choo choo

Choo choo choo choo choo choo choo choo
It's PPE we need you see

Choo choo choo choo choo choo choo choo
Choo choo choo choo choo choo choo choo
Choo choo choo choo choo choo choo choo
It's PPE we need you see.
The Permanent Secretary revealed in a Select Committee that non-participation in EU Procurements for needed supplies was a political decision, before changing his account later.

Ultracrepidate

Now here's a new word – "ULTRACREPIDATE"" -
- To exceed your scope and articulate.
Like when Mister #ShortCummings
Tries to impact the runnings
Of scientists that he can't emulate.

Stay in Your House or Flat

By Peter Cashman
Inspired by: Men in Black

Whoo
Stay in your house or flat
It's Covid-19, uhh, though it can't be seen.
Stay in your house or flat *(house or flat)*
It's important to remember
Yes yes yes.

Socialise from your flat, remember that.
Don't want to meet you face to face. Remote contact.
Houseparty, pictionary
See the thing I draw, say what you see
So don't think you can pop to the shops
Each day for the things that you want
If you go out, keep your distance
We can't get close 'cause we got no resistance.
And check in each day with the government brief
Big it up for Chris Witty, the medical chief
These times are strange, but we've got your back.
Gotta stick to these rules, stay in your house or flat.

Uh and
Stay home and just kick back *(just kick back)*
Clear your agenda *(oooh,oooh, oooh)*
Take care and know the facts. *(know the facts)*
They're crucial to remember *(crucial to remember)*

Uh uh, uh uh, now
From the youngest to the oldest guys.
Loads of feelings, laughs, cries, tonnes of lows, highs.
Lift the gloom, it's not impending doom,
Smile and like *BOOM* laughter fills the room up.
Shopping manic, don't need no panicking.
You will find the, sanitiser.
The deliveries, of your groceries,
Will mostly bring the cheese that you need.
Do what we say, this is a common cause.

Keyworkers?
I hear the neighbour's roars and applause for ya
You're our first, last and only line of defence
We love the doctors and the local nurse.
So do cheer them, revere them,
If they ever shed tears then,
Calm fears and, thank the peerless
Hospitals, takin' on all the stress
Show your thanks for the N H S

Stay in
Your house or flat
Stay in
Your house or flat
You can crash on the couch like me, the couch like me, the couch like me c'mon *(couch with me)*
Let me see ya facetime with me, facetime with me, facetime with me c'mon *(facetime, time, time)*

Let me see ya have a talk with me, just talk with me,
Have a talk with me
'Til you get bad network
And freeze *(uh huh huh ha)*

Stay home. Try to relax. *(try to relax)*
But don't have an all-day bender *(oooh,oooh, oooh)*
Take care and know the facts. *(know the facts)*
They're vital to remember *(no, no)*

All right check it, your rights may have been restricted,
I know you might feel conflicted.
But trust me, if you have a moments reflection,
Then you'll see it's for your own protection.
So, stay in your home and behind that door
Cause it don't care if you're rich or poor.
Don't risk any lives, forget those travel plans.
Be wise with what you choose. It's time to stay in,
Time to stay in.

Stay with your dog or cat *(they're your chums)*
Browse an online vendor *(buy yourself a blender)*
Take care and know the facts. *(and tell your mum)*
They're crucial to remember *(crucial to remember)*
Stay in your house or flat *(they're your chums)*
Clear your agenda *(oooh, oooh, oooh)*
Take care and know the facts.
They're vital to remember .

Off his “R”s

It seems that it's now quite a farce;
He blusters and bluffs and blah-blahs.
But here's my reflection -
He misleads on infection
Each time that he gets off his "R"s.

More Dense

Some commentators explained the higher number of deaths in the UK by explaining that the UK population is more dense

So let us not sit on the fence.
Let’s apply some robust common sense;
Though we’ve more deaths than planned,
This you can understand
When you know that our leader’s more dense.

We're still waiting

Inspired by: *I'm Still Waiting.*

I remember when
You spoke for Leave in referendum,
And for PM you would try
You could always try to lie,
They believed you.

Then one day we heard
There was Russian interference,
You wouldn't take the blame
And then you lied again,
When you said
"Dominic
You must wait for me
Wait patiently; report
Someday it will be published.
Ooh Dominic,
You must wait for me.
Wait patiently; report
Someday it will be published!"

And we're still waiting.
Ooh, we're waiting
Ooh, still waiting
Are we just fools? Are we just fools?

(Are we just fools to keep waiting?)
To keep waiting (Are we just fools?)
For truth. (Are we just fools ?)
Ooh, we're waiting. (Are we just fools?)
We're still waiting (Are we just fools to keep waiting?)
For truth. (Are we just fools ?)
For truth. (Are we just fools?)
Then Grayling finally came.
He said he would be chairman
Of the Intelligence;
Didn't seem to make much sense.
And still the report's not published.
Like a man without a book
We had to face the truth
We were still without report.
Boris said:
"Citizens, You must wait for me
Wait patiently; report
Someday it will be published,
Ooh citizens, You must wait for me
Wait patiently; report
Someday it will be published."
And we're still waiting.

Report has never shown its face
Since the day it was ready for your name

You turn the page to empty space. Redact?
But it's that report we're waiting for.

Don't you know we're waiting
(Are we just fools to keep waiting?)
We're waiting to read
The truth, I miss it (Are we just fools to keep waiting?)
We're waiting. (Are we just fools?)
Stop redacting. (Are we just fools?)
Redact? Redact? Redact? No!
(Are we just fools to keep waiting?)
We need to read. (Are we just fools?)
And we want to read. (Are we just fools?)
That's what our friends say. (Are we just fools?)
Are we fooled? (Are we just fools?)
(to keep waiting?) ……

Complete Wifi

My laptop's like a TV now;
It works in every room.
If I've not got my trousers on,
You can't see that on Zoom.

Ill with covid

Inspired by "Ill Wind"

August 2020

I once had a virus, I tried to ignore it,
And go like before to the pub and the shop.
Let's say we've a strategy, we were all for it -
To kill off some old folk and then it would stop.

Control the herds;
I had to develop a strategy.
Cajole - three words -
Was the way that I'd done this before.

So simply found
To give a sound
A beautiful soundbite rich and round

Oh the time I spent with Dom
before we found out we were wrong, we were wrong, we were wrong.
For herd immunity
Impunity
It wasn't in fact the case;
I'd said "Brace, Brace"
But the strategy was missing.

Oh what else can I ban?

Haven't you, hasn't anyone got a plan?
Oh what else can I ban?
Oh, what a blow, now I know, I can't get away with a no-show ?

Who's got a plan?
There must be one
When was it done?

Well we've got the Sage experts
Though we may ignore them
Suppressing their words
If they don't support us
For every day,
In a podium way,
They'll be hidden away
Like the words on a bus.

I've got no plan
The outcomes I'm seeking unknown to me
I've got no plan. got no plan, made a plan, man.

There's not much hope of getting a plan
Though I'd willingly pay Dom a ton

I know some expert folk, some textbook folk
And pretending to do what they say

Gone away! Gone away!
Now an ambulance took me away.

Will you kindly think of some plan?
Now what the devil is next to ban?

Let's bring in the Police
I want some great plan done
I see the numbers - more and more and more.
Without that plan,
I'm seeing we'll go down the pan

I had manifesto, I wanted to scrap it,
Displaying my talents at ditching a plan.
But early this year when I did not defer
There's just one thing that I would prefer.
I've got to do Brexit and wanted our exit
And nothing else mattered to me
I've got to do Brexit and wanted our exit
And nothing else mattered to me

The voters still give their support
What if I don't do what I ought? -
I think I'll abolish the Court.

Golf in wartime: Onward Richmond Golfers?

Inspired by*: "Onward Christian Soldiers"*

Also inspired by the 1940 rules of the Richmond Golf Club which explained how to continue a golf game in time of war

17 March 2020

1 Onward Richmond golfers
Golfing through the war,
Shifting bits of shrapnel
If they're on the floor.
Any other bomb splinters
You must intervene;
Pick it up and bring it back
To save mowing machine.

2 During competitions
When you're on the spot,
You may please take cover
If you're being shot.
Should the bombs be falling,
Grab a cup of tea.
You can temporarily cease
Without a penalty.

3 We have put a red flag up
So, the place we've showed -
Where there are explosives
That will soon explode.
Well, it's more or less a mark
Of the range of bomb.
It could well be a safe distance
Measured out therefrom.

4 Splinters on the fairway
If they're near your ball
May be moved quite freely
With no charge at all.
Should you find that shrapnel piece
Could your ball collide,
If this is by accident,
It will have a free ride.

5 If your ball in normal play
Comes under attack
And the bullets knock it off
You may put it back.
Should the bastards damage it
Quite beyond repair,
Drop another ball, but please ensure it's
No nearer, that's fair.

6 Balls that fall in bomb craters
Causing them to stop? -
Ok to retrieve them;
You may lift and drop.
Though must not be nearer
Than before to hole,
Keeping to the line you shot
From fairway to flagpole

7 Now suppose you take your shot
While you do, you're bombed
This may put you off your stroke.
Do not feel wronged.
You can have another go.
We're reasonable folk.
All you'll lose for that explosion -
One penalty stroke.

Act 2: Expedition

The Ballad of Dom and Bojo

Inspired by: *"Ballad of John and Yoko"*

May 2020

Meeting all the Covid-ill patients,
Shaking hands 'because I'm a clown.
The bug with no drug said
"I'm on to your lungs";
Unlike Dom, haven't even got out of town.
But you know we've left EC -
No clue how hard it can be.
The way things are going,
They're going to beautify me.

Finally got a bed in the ward then.
Tommy's nurses all very nice.
Some of them skittish,
Even not British;
When this is over I think I'll tax them twice.
But you know we've left EC -
No clue how hard it can be.
The way things are going,
They're going to beautify me.

Instead of me lying with Dom in the street,
Lying in the ward - what a pair.
The newspapers said

"Say what're you doing in bed";
I said "I'm only trying to get me some air".
But you know we've left EC -
No clue how hard it can be.
The way things are going,
They're going to beautify me.

Carrie she then managed a baby day,
Being Dad I can do, now number ten.
Last night Carrie said
"Oh boy when you're dead
There'll be no lying with you, where's your soul then?"

Made a little trip out to Chequers;
Sudoku and telly all day.
Then I met Raab,
As I left him in charge;
Nothing happened while I was away.
But you know we've left EC -
No clue how hard it can be.
The way things are going,
They're going to beautify me.

Dom drove a long way to Durham,
Broke many rules in one go.
Well that is long runnings
From Mister Short Cummings

I guess those rules he didn't know
But you know we've left EC -
No clue how hard it can be.
The way things are going,
They're going to beautify me.
The way things are going,
They will beatify me.

"Do Nothing"? but failed

I think you thought you had it nailed,
Your cunning plan; what it entailed
Was do nothing but flight,
And then stay out of sight.
In that task you undoubtedly failed.

I Don't Beg Pardon

Inspired by "Rose Garden"
(and fairy stories told in a Rose Garden)
May 2020

I don't beg pardon.
I'm talking bollocks in the rose garden.
Along with covid drip,
There's gotta be a little road trip.
When in London cannot cope,
There's no care no hope,
So you go oh oh oh oh
I don't beg pardon.
I'm talking bollocks in the rose garden.

I could promise you the truth,
Though I may be uncouth,
But you won't hear travel tales that I'm a rover.
So you'd better think it over.
Now I'm sweet-talking you and some of it's true.
I would bring North the bug back then as a great infector.
You can call me Vector.
So I confess to the Press but don't say sorry.
You shouldn't be so melancholy.
Who are you? But ask your questions while you can

I don't beg pardon
I'm talking bollocks in the rose garden.

Along with covid drip,
There's gotta be a little road trip.

I don't beg pardon
I'm talking bollocks in the rose garden.
I could spin you a talk, how we'd all go for a walk
But if that's what the neighbours saw
As I heard you had a witness
Then we were walking for our fitness

Check eyesight before you drive
Just to stay alive,
And some reasonable folk
May think I'm a rascal,
But I went to Barnard Castle.

It was good in the woods, I won't say sorry.
After today I'm not your quarry.
Who are you? But ask your questions while you can.

I must now exit.
I'm got some bollocks for the "No's" Brexit
We're talking in real-time
There's got to be a "No Deal" sometime.

Was it b*ll**ks spoken in the Rose Garden?

See the relevant www.viewdelta.blogspot.com entries

Stand By Your Dom

Inspired by: Stand By Your Man

May 2020

Sometimes it's hard to be the PM,
Giving all your work to just one man.
There's knock down times, and poor lock down times,
With Durham journeys that weren't planned.
But if you need him, you'll forgive him,
Though Steve Baker doesn't understand.
And at the briefings, oh then you must back him,
'Cause after all Dom is your man.

Stand by your Dom,
Give the country two fingers,
And some old instinct claptrap,
You'll hope no mem'ry lingers.
Stand by your Dom, and show the rest your contempt,
He doesn't need to stick to plan.
Stand by your man.
Stand by your Dom, and show that he is exempt.
Keep talking all the crap you can.
Stand by your man.

Barnard Castle – Dom's Ditty

By Fred Cashman

May 2020

I drove to Barnard Castle
To see if I could see.
I strapped my nipper in the back
And in went wife Mary.
I didn't have my glasses,
At least I knew the way –
Just a shame that I'd forgot
it was my wife's birthday.

Barnard Castle, Barnard Castle,
Out there in the sticks.
No better place to test your eyes
Than on A66.

We came into the town itself –
Don't think I caused a crash.
We stopped just at the river
And I heard a little splash.
I thought perhaps I should get out
And bring the family.
The advice was just to 'stay at home',
But that's for plebs, not me.

Barnard Castle, Barnard Castle,
Bluebells among the sticks.

No better place to test your eyes
Than on A66.

We wandered by the river,
Shared our COVID-19.
We would have gotten away with it
If we had not been seen.
See, I didn't go round the castle
Nor about the town,
So I actually did stick to
My own version of lockdown

Barnard Castle, Barnard Castle,
With people do not mix.
No better place to test your eyes
Than on A66.

On our journey back to home –
Road lines a little blurry –
The little nipper shouted out
"we're stopping for a pee".
I said "Well, that's unusual,
It rarely happens so."
We'd just travelled 2-60 miles,
None of us had to go.

Barnard Castle, Barnard Castle,
I'm not one of them.
No better place to have a wee

Than by the A1(M).

We headed out into the woods
And had a little play.
You see, we had to celebrate,
For it was Easter day.
While wondering out there I said
"Oh shit, think we've been seen –
But these guys they will keep schtum,
They wouldn't be so mean".

Barnard Castle, Barnard Castle
Not good for politics.
No better place to test your eyes
Than on A66.

Six weeks and Barnard story broke.
The press left me bereft.
Thank God PM denied it as from
The campaigning left.
But then had to give a statement –
Could do without the hassle –
But won't say I shouldn't a-feckin'-gone
Out in Barnard Castle.

Barnard Castle, Barnard Castle,
Got me in a fix.
No better place to test your eyes
Than on A66.

Extra Homes of Durham

Inspired by "Stately Homes of England"
May 2020

The Wakefield lass,
The Cummings Lad,
In fact, whole family,
We have, despite all cups of tea,
Great urinary capacity;
Here you see the three of us;
That may be all you see of us,
For in Durham we will hide,
Sister will bring a mess of pottage
Delivered to the extra cottage,
I'll emphasise this quite heavily,
As we in fact you'll never see
Though we should not be there now,
Lock us down would be unfair now,
As to one home we'd then be tied.
We are the leaders,
So we have this power abundant,
To drive from London.
Instinct will be our guide.

1. The extra homes of Durham
How handily they stand
To prove the upper classes
Have still the upper hand;

Though the fact that there is
No plans consent,
And to pay Council Tax
There's no intent,
Is not something we'll repent,
Or apologise.
I'm certain won't spoil the fun
Of me the darling son.
And to that home I can drive
Without needing to pee.
I made the journey alive,
Though broke the rules, P.C.
And yes you might think
I'd lose my job.
With conduct they'd reject,
Except
For the extra homes of Durham

2. The extra homes of Durham
Contained we Cummings three.
And so we made our food there,
And we at last could pee.
There's a kitchen we can
Make models in,
All indoors where we don't
Meet our kin,
And a lavatory where we've been,
Yes, quite urgently;

Oh yes we had to go;
For four hours staunched the flow.
This cottage self-contained now -
A unit on its own.
It’s wise not to declare it;
Or Tax bills will be shown.
But still if they ever
Catch us out,
Which with any luck they won’t,
We don’t
Pay the Council Tax to Durham.

3. The extra homes of Durham,
Are the best place to wait.
Or just a little stroll now,
But stay on Dad’s estate.
And from hospital,
If you’re going home,
You can’t get a taxi
Without a phone,
And can’t do this alone,
So you phone up Dom,
And then I will drive the car,
Don’t go very far.
If we’re seen by a neighbour.
Just say he can’t exist.
Or else he votes for Labour,
So “nonsense” we insist.

If anyone spots
Us, joins the dots,
Say we're not in a crowd,
We're proud
Of the extra homes of Durham.

4. The extra homes of Durham
Provide a useful base
From which we can manoeuvre,
And move from place to place.
Though the drive to London
Is very far,
And the eyesight is dodgy
For the car,
I don't think that will mar
Half-hour eyesight test
For Mary's birthday bash,
The Barnard Castle dash.
Our duty to the nation
Is not to make a fuss.
Won't give full explanation;
Rules are for them, not us.
We don't need to fight,
Mary can write,
And that's how the nation learned,
We weren't
In the extra homes of Durham.

5. The extra homes of Durham
Did not go quite to plan
Our presence widely noticed
The shit has hit the fan.
There may be more sightings,
Oh please not more;
We've given excuses
For three or four,
And that is all, I swore;
They've accepted it.
Don't mention GSK,
I've had enough today.,
The Ministers have tweeted
We didn't leave the place;
Or people who we greeted
Aren't germane to the case.
The Government's crashed.
And the message trashed,
And other points we've ducked,
We're................ plucked
From the extra homes of Durham.

The Council Tax issue was identified by Alex Tiffin of Black Isle Journalism: https://universalcreditsuffer.com/2020/06/11/cummings-lockdown-cottage-visited-by-council-for-council-tax-avoidance/

Extra Homes of Durham – Addendum

Inspired by "Stately Homes of England"
Witnesses claim to have seen Mr Cummings walking in the woods near Durham a week after Easter. How could this be, when Cummings had already demonstrated to the Prime Minister that his phone had been in London during that time, and the phone certainly had not driven up the M1 on its own?

So, we explore here the entirely hypothetical possibility that Dominic Cummings drove South alone on Easter Monday, and that a hypothetical phone was left with a hypothetical aide in London, while the hypothetically travelling Dominic Cummings drove back in a hypothetical car up the hypothetical M1 to hypothetical Durham.

The weeks go by,
My frauds they spy,
But I've got off scot free.
Though the challenge tends to harden,
I fixed a conference in the Garden.
Here you heard me blathering
About my Durham gathering,
And my half-hour eye drive test.
The evidence was on my phone
That it did not drive back alone,
And though you may think it's sinister
I did fool the Prime Minister,
Though I asked him not to show it

The alibi – best not to blow it,
Don't want the story to be bust.
I am Controller
Of this land that's led by muppets;
They are my puppets;
Nothing could be more just.

6. The extra homes of Durham
Departing from them when,
I first returned to London,
And then went back again,
And though I was careful
To leave a phone,
Collecting some "evidence"
Lest they moan,
In London that was shown
To Prime Minister
Who didn't pass it on,
Not to rely upon.
My wife said I'm in London;
Well Durham's what she meant.
But all's well on the run down,
So back up North I went.
And maybe I should
Have missed the wood,
Verification's very good,
I could
Be in extra homes of Durham.

One Rule for You, One Rule for Me

Inspired by "One Rule for You"

May 2020

What kind of line is that when you say
You're not limited by normal rules?
You tell us all these things, you changed your blog
And act as if you think we're fools
What kind of line is that, your fantasy?
One rule for you, one rule for me
I know your Barnard Castle story
But you shouldn't say such stupid things
And people are amazed our leader
To this eyesight nonsense he clings
What kind of line is that, your fantasy
One rule for you, one rule for me.

You may believe in what you like
But why don't you keep Covid to yourself
We say what we know is right
And that these rules are set up for our health
What kind of line is that, your fantasy
One rule for you, one rule for me
One rule for you, one rule for me.

Dominic's checking his eyesight

Inspired by "Teddy Bears' Picnic"

May 2020

If you go down to the woods today
You're sure of a big surprise
When Dom , who's s'posed to be locked away
Is looking you in the eyes
You didn't think in Durham he was
No need to be embarrassed because
Today's the day that
Dom'nic's checking his eyesight.

Eyesight test for Dominic,
As all the Cummings clan are having
A woodland walk today.
Watch them, catch them unawares,
And see them strolling on their holiday.
See them gaily gad about
The lockdown rules they shout;
They never have any cares.
And in the morning the Mummy and Daddy
Will all drive back down South
For our contracts they want fair shares.

Every Cummings to follow the rules
Decides things in their own way,
And that is why our Dominic

Is dodging the P'lice today,
Beneath the trees where nobody sees
They'll break the rules as much as they please
'Cause that's the way that
Dominic checks his eyesight

Eyesight test for Dominic
Though Mary thinks she's lying
In London home today.
Watch them, catch them unawares
And tell the Guardian they're hiding away.
See them drive A66;
The contracts they can fix,
With never a tender care.
And in the morning you'll see the Daddy
Will then drive back down South.
While the people do not dare.
While the people do not dare.

If you go down to the shops today

Inspired by "Teddy Bears' Picnic"
June 2020

If you go down to the shops today
You're better go in disguise
As butler to the Earl of Strathmore,
You've got to evade the spies.
For every Lord, a sighting is scored
Though buying the papers was all you thought
Today's the day Queen's relative's in the papers.

Atticus for Kinghorne Earl.
He joins with Dominic as spotted
In Durham out today,
Watch them, catch them unawares.
And see them strolling on their holiday.
See them gaily gad about.
The lockdown rules they flout;
They walk around so carefree.
And in the morning the police are calling
To say that it's appalling.
And the Earl thinks "Back to Dundee"

Every toff who won't follow the rules
Decides things in their own way,
And that is why the noble Lord
Is dodging the P'lice today.

Beneath the trees where nobody sees
He'll break the rules as much as he'll please;
'Cause that's the way the
Queen's relative's in the papers.

Atticus for Kinghorne Earl
Although the Queen Mum's cousin is
At his second home today,
Watch him, catch him unawares.
As he sends his butler on his way
See his Scottish highland reel.
And "Instinct" s what he'll feel
When he decides what's fair
And on the morrow the Earl of Strathmore
Hopes they'll let him back in
While the people do not dare,
While the people do not dare.

From The Sunday Times, "Atticus": What is it about the Barnard Castle area that lures people out of lockdown? First it was Dominic Cummings, and now the 19th Earl of Strathmore and Kinghorne has been visited by Durham police after arriving in the area from his home in Glamis Castle, near Dundee.

And what are the rules?

It turns out that there was no problem....

DomCummings 28/05/2020 00:05:00
Inserted:
, unless you need to check your eyesight, in which case a 60-mile round trip to a tourist attraction with the family, a walk by the river and a walk in the woods is fine.

.gov.uk

What You Can and Cannot Do

You should not drive for exercise, unless you need to check your eyesight, in which case a 60-mile round trip to a tourist attraction with the family, a walk by the river and a walk in the woods is fine.

Will he Stay or Will He Go?

By Paul Shrimpton

Inspired by: "Should I Stay or Should I Go?"

May 2020

Boris, you got to let us know
Will he stay or will he go?
If you say that he is fine
You're buggered 'til the end of time
So you got to let us know
Will he stay or will he go?

It's always lies, lies, lies
You're happy telling porky pies
But then he drove up north and back
And now you want us off your back
Well, come on and let us know
Will he stay or will he go?

Should he stay or should he go now?
Should he stay or should he go now?
If he goes, you're still in trouble
But if he stays it will be double
So come on and let us know

This bad decision's bugging us
(esta indecisión me molesta)
It's like you wrote it on a bus
(si no me quieres, librarme)
Exactly what does lockdown mean?

(dígame que tengo ser)
Don't try to justify his bullshit
(sabes que ropa me quedra)
Come on and let us know
(me tienes que decir)
Should he be sacked or will YOU go?
(me debo ir o quedarme)

Should he stay or should he go now?
(yo me enfrió o lo soplo)
Should he stay or should he go now?
(yo me enfrió o lo soplo)
If he goes, you're still in trouble
(si me voy va a haber peligro)
But if he stays it will be double
(si me quedo sera el doble)
So ya gotta let us know
(me tienes que decir)
Should he be sacked or will YOU go?
(me debo ir o quedarme)

Should he stay or should he go now?
(tengo frío por los ojos)
If he goes, you're still in trouble
(si me voy va a haber peligro)
But if he stays it will be double
(si me quedo sera el doble)
So ya gotta let us know
(me tienes que decir)
Will he stay or will he go?

Old Durham Town

by Peter Cook

Inspired by: "Old Durham Town"

CHORUS: I've got to leave old Durham town,
I've got to leave old Durham town.
Dom's got to leave old Durham town,
Cos that Brexit's gonna get me down.

Back in twenty one and six
I remember Cam'run running out the door.
Bojo told me he was going to war, he was lying,
Lying, lying, lying, lying lie.

CHORUS: I've got to leave old Durham town, etc

When I was a boy, I spent my time,
Building cars and fishing on the foggy Tyne.
Watching Nissan Leafs cumming down the line,
Now they're leaving,
Leaving, leafing, leafing, leafing me.

CHORUS: I've got to leave old Durham town, etc

The last week Mama passed away,
Covid, son, was all she'd say.
Dominic Cummings took my breath away, so I'm leaving,
Leaving, leaving, leaving, leaving free.

CHORUS: Dom's got to leave old Durham Town

Act 3: Prevention

Heroes, Just for One day

Inspired by: *“Heroes”*

May 2020

I, I won’t get hurt
And you, you’ll be alert
Though nothing will keep kids away
We can teach them, just for one day
We can be Heroes, just for one day

And you, with no PPE
And I, I'll walk carefully
Coronavirus, and this is a fact
It is infectious, protection is lacked
Though crowding will keep us together
We could cheat science, just for one day
We can be Heroes, for ever and ever
What d'you say?

I, I wish you’d survive
Like the rich folk, you would stay alive
Though crowding, crowding will keep us together
We can’t beat it , for ever and ever
Oh we can be Heroes, just for one day

I, I won't get hurt
And you, you'll be alert
Though nothing will keep kids away
We can teach them, just for one day
We can be Heroes, just for one day

I, I can remember (I remember)
The kids in the class (in the class)
And they all stay well apart (well apart)
No kids kissed, they just worked on 3 Rs.(worked on 3 Rs)

And the leaders, just sat on their R's
We can't beat it , for ever and ever
Oh we can be Heroes, just for one day

We can be Heroes
Mustn't score zeroes
We can be Heroes
Just for one day
We can be Heroes

We're nothing, and nothing will help us
Maybe they're lying, then we better not stay
But could we be safer, just for one day

Oh-oh-oh-ohh, oh-oh-oh-ohh
Just for one day.

Second Wave

Inspired by: "Second Wave"!

June 2020

We're all in Lockdown,
I wonder how you can dare go out now,
We're still stuck here now,
Do bother whether you've got a mask?
How can you think you are protected wherever we go?
Take notice of the risks now.

Stay calm and watch out for infection.
You know we're not going away.
We all had the time for reflection.
It starts when we go out to play,
To stay we'll encounter resistance.
Just call me and get me on zoom.
Keep on, we are at social distance,
Even when we're in the room.

'Cause you know the danger's real for all.
(Let's never transmit it)
Needing help? Then you must call.
(Lets never transmit it)
So you want to play it cool.
We're always isolating.

I know it's tantalising.
So, tell me what I have to do.

Stay home (and never transmit it).
(Let's never transmit it).
Work Home
(that's if it's possible).
You keep safe.
I'm always worried 'bout a
Second wave.

Wash your hands both, front and back;
Can you sing while you're washing?
Twenty seconds, birthday song,
You just sing while you're sloshing.

How can you think you are protected wherever we go?
Take notice of the risks now.

Stay calm and wait in for the broadcast.
You know we're not going away.
We all know the better we follow,
The sooner we'll all get to play.
No-one is above these clear rules now.
Watch out for an example.
I found out when we heard from the garden
Some will not follow the rules.

'Cause you know the danger's real for all.
(Let's never transmit it).
Needing help? Then you must call
(Let's never transmit it).
So you want to play it cool
We're always isolating.

I know it's tantalising.
So tell me what I have to do
Let's never transmit it)

Stay home (and never transmit it).
(Let's never transmit it).
Work Home
(that's if it's possible).
You keep safe.
I'm always worried 'bout a
Second wave.

Stay home (and never transmit it).
(Let's never transmit it).
Work Home
(that's if it's possible).
You keep safe.
I'm always worried 'bout a
Second wave.

Things that would astonish you

Inspired by "Sentry Song" by W.S. Gilbert (from "Iolanthe")

June 2020

We looked at renovating this 1882 piece, and for many parts of the structure we did that, but we found the second verse ("When in that House M.P.'s divide,…") to be in perfect working order and so left it untouched (except for revising "No man" to "No one"), and some other areas needed very little work to update them.

When all day long a chap remains
In queues to vote, to solve monotony
He exercises of his brains,
That is, assuming that he's got any.
Though some are nurtured in the laps
Of luxury, yet I admonish you,
You'll find some intellectual chaps
Who think of things that would astonish you.

Rees-Mogg's not just an ornament
--Fal, lal, la!
For he can deal with resistance
--Fal, lal, la! La
And each member in the argument
That tries to do social distance
Must either queue round Parliament
Or else have remote existence.

When in that House M.P.'s divide,
If they've a brain and cerebellum, too,
They've got to leave that brain outside,
And vote just as their leaders tell 'em to.
But then the prospect of a lot
Of dull M. P.'s in close proximity,
All thinking for themselves, is what
No one can face with equanimity.

So Silly Walk , our tournament
Fal la--Fal la!
Rees Mogg can deal with resistance
--Fal, lal, la! La la
And each member in the argument
That tries to do social distance
Must either queue round Parliament
Or else have remote existence
Fal lal la!, la la
Must either queue round Parliament
Or else have remote existence
Fal lal la!, la la.

Alo Vera

Inspired by "Football's Coming Home"

Peter Cook planned a campaign to chart his catchy song "Alo Vera" on 18th June.
This turned out to be exactly the day that was appropriate to pay tribute to Dame Vera Lynn, who is mentioned in the song.

'Alo Vera Lynn
Don't know where u have bin
I've bin fightin' Brexit with Victory Gin
Soon we will be fruit pickin
Cos we are the Brexit fishermin'

It's comin' 'ome, it's comin' 'ome
Brexit's comin' 'ome
It's comin' 'ome, it's comin' 'ome
And the nurses are goin' 'ome

Que sera sera, what will be will be
Some will live, some will die
But I've got a passport, a coin and a tie
While Boris tells another pork pie
I leave the snowflakes to cry
From Nigel Farridge to Bobby Moore
48 : 52 we knew the score
After Corona we want more

It's gonna be just like the War

It's comin' 'ome, it's comin' 'ome
Brexit's comin' 'ome
It's comin' 'ome, it's comin' 'ome
I'm home alone
And my hair I cannot comb

It's comin' 'ome, it's comin' 'ome
Brexit's comin' 'ome
It's comin' 'ome, it's comin' 'ome
I'm home alone
And I can't afford a scone

I'm not a remona
We drink the Corona
We are the doctors, nurses, scientific persona
We are the Brexit land army .. from Verona
We fear no ill for we have Bojona
'Alo Vera, All Cor Blimey
We're gonna take back control of Old Blighty
The M20's blocked all nighty
But Bulldog Spirits gonna make it alrighty
If you just take off your nighty ...

It's comin' 'ome, it's comin' 'ome
Brexit's comin' 'ome

It's comin' 'ome, it's comin' 'ome
And I got Corona in a care 'ome

It's comin' 'ome, it's comin' 'ome
Brexit's comin' 'ome
It's comin' 'ome, it's comin' 'ome
And I can't afford a scone

It's comin' 'ome, it's comin' 'ome
Brexit's comin' 'ome
It's comin' 'ome, it's comin' 'ome
And the nurses are goin' 'ome

It's comin' 'ome, it's comin' 'ome
Brexit's comin' 'ome
It's comin' 'ome, it's comin' 'ome
I'm home alone
And my hair I cannot comb

Shifting the Blame

I'm not sure he has any shame.
We can see his disgraceful new game
"Not the time?" Is it now
That he figures out how
He can start to be shifting the blame?

A Song of Idiotic Prejudice

Inspired by: *"A Song of Patriotic Prejudice"*

August 2020

* The asterisked Lines are examples of what can be declaimed (or claimed) between verses, in Flanders and Swann style).

Our system, our system, our system is best.
The system's world-beating, outclasses the rest.

* "Typical Tory understatement"

100k people we will test each day,
Which was kind of awkward, so what can we say?
100k tests then is what we like most,
As thirty-nine thousand are put in the post.

* "Well, it all counts, doesn't it!... never mind if they're lost or not"

Though Apple and Google thought they had an App
It wasn't our system, so we thought it's crap.
It wouldn't supply us with data all right,
And ours nearly worked on the Isle of Wight.

Our system, our system is best.
The system's world-beating, outclasses the rest.

* "Oh, bring in the old Dido and don't let's talk about the App"

And then Dido Harding, the tracers she'd teach,
As she set the record for worst data breach,
She used to run Talktalk, incompetent crew,
To judge by my dealings, so how about you?

Our system was brilliant, so give it a clap.
Since we're scrapping the app,we will call it a wrap.

* "Call for Tracers! Who's good at watching Netflix?"

And twenty five thousand new tracers she'd get.
Unneeded political target was met.
They twiddled their fingers, they twiddled their thumbs.
They're paid to watch Netflix and sit on their bums..

And we'll set examples for you to take note.
Please don't do as we do, we're not in the same boat.
In your case if there's second home that you own.
You still must remain in the first one alone.

Our system is noble, our system is good,
And clever, expensive and misunderstood.

And all the world over, comparing the stats.
You'll see that we are demonstrably prats;
We argue with experts, we may call a halt,
But be in no doubt that all failure's your fault.

Our system, our system is best;
The system's world-beating, outclasses the rest.

You may think we're wicked or naturally bad;
But please do not say so, Eat Out and be glad,

Our system, our system is best
And the source of the system is Dom'nic
Boris
Dom'nic
Boris
And me .....

With no tender

Inspired by: Love Me Tender

November 2020

Many of these songs are written within a day or two of the relevant events. This one is an exception. I kept a folder of relevant stories, meaning to work them all into a song "With No Tender". By the time I came to write it I realised that the song would be impossibly long if all the cases were included – and so the lyrics include a selection.
If you want to know more about the subject of this song, the best way to get an up-to-date briefing is probably to search online for "The Good Law Project" which is seeking to challenge the contract awards by judicial review. The extent of crony contracting became apparent later in 2020 with a report from the National Audit Office.

With no tender, with no checks,
Funding still extends.
Lord knows who is favoured next;
Contracts to their friends.

With no tender, PPE,
That is to Pestfix,
Allocated carefully,
By whose arse he licks.

Millions for a crucial mask.
Have the spec they read?
Sadly they forgot to ask,

Fasten round your head?

Billions wasted on duff kit.
Profits still are banked.
Those who left us in the shit -
Seemingly they're ranked.

What's Ayanda's competence?
Set up yesterday;
Let's forget Due Diligence,
In a rush to pay.

Gove's directing this shit-storm -
"Standing have you none" -
(How he tried to block Jo Maugham
Hiding what they've done).

But to court our heroes go,
As the stakes are upped,
Now Good Law Project can show
How this was corrupt.

With no tender, with no skill,
Corruption we have seen,
Leaving UK much more ill;
Now please buy vaccine.

Outgoing Man

20 August 2020

The Government that said "This is not the time to allocate blame" seemed to temporarily forgot that they had said that and to gain some sudden insights.

For Public Health, something is lacking,
Despite Matthew Hancock's full backing
For the outgoing man
Who was not told the plan
Before Hancock told Press of his sacking.

The start of Duncan Selbie's message to PHE colleagues on Sunday 16 August:
Dear everyone
I am sorry beyond words at the way that decisions about our future have been briefed to the media before I have had the chance to explain them......

Act 4: Distraction

Oven-Ready Deal is Over

Inspired by: *When the Carnival is Over*

There was an earlier version of this song in 2017 covering Barnier and May's interactions, but in view of the backward progress since that time an update seemed appropriate.

2 July 2020

Say goodbye our former friends now,
Not much progress, I believe.
As we all see how this ends now -
Fifty-two who said we'd Leave.

Brexit Done? Won't take a minute.
Oven-ready, we were told.
Story's busted now we're in it.
Once again, it's oversold.

Worked for months, in each new meeting,
Not much done, as time goes by.
But the joys of deal are fleeting.
Ready Deal? Pie in the sky.

Many billion is the bill now;
Our reactions are quite mixed.
Is this still the People's Will now?
Let's pretend that Ireland's fixed.

Level terms? I think that those'll
Be left up to David Frost.
He'll say "No" to each proposal.
So that "No Deal" won't be lost

In the Parliaments they'll judge it;
Bluff and bluster, PMQs.
Implementing, they will fudge it,
It's the people who will lose.

This is all a big investment;
Hope that no-one harbours doubt.
Not for us, impact assessment;
Let's just see how it turns out.

Every problem, now we'll park it;
Doesn't matter, let's just Leave.
Please don't mention Single Market.
Auld Lang Syne, on New Year's Eve.
Please don't mention Single Market.
Auld Lang Syne, on New Year's Eve.

I'm Telling a Terrible Story

Inspired by: *I'm Telling a Terrible Story, Pirates of Penzance*

PRIME MINISTER
I've been telling a terrible story,
But that doesn't diminish my glory;
For I would have lost all the floaters
That we needed as voters.
With trade we will increase the friction
The idea of improvement was fiction
This is not in the same category
As telling a regular terrible story.

[OPPOSITION MPs]
As he's telling a terrible story
He doesn't deserve any glory,
Well never mind all his cavorting
Where's the Russian reporting?
With trade he will increase the friction
The idea of improvement was fiction
This is just in the same category
As telling a regular terrible story
With trade he will increase the friction
The idea of improvement was fiction
This is just in the same category

[GOVERNMENT MPs]
He's telling a bit of a story,
But we still believe in his glory;
I know we're approaching the deadlines
We stull gave our redlines.

On trade we will increase the friction
The idea of improvement was fiction
This is roughly the same category
As telling a regular terrible story
On trade we will increase the friction
The idea of improvement was fiction
This is roughly the same category

As telling a regular terrible story..

As telling a regular terrible story

PRIME MINISTER

I've been telling a terrible story,
But that doesn't diminish my glory;
But the headlines manipulate maybe
With a new Boris baby.
The voters can surely not fire us
They need us like coronavirus.
Remember you must trust a Tory
Who's telling a regular terrible story.

[OPPOSITION MPs]

Well he's telling a terrible story.
He doesn't deserve any glory,
And he's grabbed all the headlines; maybe
They're fixed on the baby
And now we are left in the mire as
Poor working on coronavirus.
So never be trusting a Tory
Who's telling a regular terrible story.
And now we are left in the mire as
Poor working on coronavirus.
So never be trusting a Tory
Who's telling a regular terrible story.

[GOVERNMENT MPs]

He's telling a bit of a story,
But we still believe in his glory;
And the headlines are positive maybe
For a new Boris baby.
The voters can surely not fire us.
They need us like coronavirus.
Remember you must trust a Tory
Who's telling a regular terrible story.
The voters can surely not fire us.
They need us for coronavirus.
Remember you must trust a Tory
Who's telling a regular terrible story.

Look in your fridge

20 August 2020

No-one could find the Prime Minister

Is he stuck in a tent with a midge?
Or climbing a Scots mountain ridge?
This is somewhat sinister -
We've lost our Prime Minister.
Please everyone, look in your fridge.

On My Site

Phew! The Prime Minister was tracked down to a legally occupied cottage and illegally pitched yurt in Scotland. The Prime Minister publicly blamed the Scottish National Party for his discovery, based on one rogue tweet.

25 August 2020

The cottage is found on a high site,
But the farmer said "You've pitched on my site!"
While he was somewhat hurt
By the fire and the yurt,
I guess Johnson was testing his eyesight.

Don't Go Breaking My Yurt

Inspired by: Don't Go Breaking My Heart
Boris John and Carrie Dee
26th August 2020

Don't go breaking my yurt
It was a foolish thing.
Carrie, if I get restless
Baby, you're for the sling.
Don't go breaking my yurt
Although I climbed the fence.
Oh, farmer, I just used those two chairs
Ooh, then it got so tense.
Ooh-hoo, nobody sees us
Climbing the walls
When we're on our hols.
Ooh-hoo, nobody knows it, nobody knows.
Let's stay alert.
I made you a yurt.
Oh oh, I made you a yurt.
So don't go breaking my yurt
I won't go breaking my yurt
Don't go breaking my yurt
And nobody told us,
'Cause nobody showed us
Where the boundaries defined;
Whoa, I think we can climb it.
Please don't misunderstand me

As we must have photo op.
Oh, you put the flame to the logs
I've got Cam'ron saying "Stop" .
Ooh-hoo, nobody sees us
Climbing the walls
When we're on our hols
Ooh-hoo, nobody knows it, nobody knows
Let's stay alert
I made you a yurt
Oh oh, I made you a yurt
So don't go breaking my yurt
I won't go breaking my yurt
Don't go breaking my yurt
Ooh-hoo, nobody sees us
Climbing the walls
When we're on our hols
Let's stay alert
I made you a yurt
Oh oh, I made you a yyurt
Don't go breaking my yurt
I won't go breaking your yurt
(Don't go breaking my)
(Don't go breaking my)
Don't go breaking my yurt
(Don't go breaking my)
(Don't go breaking my)
I won't go breaking your yurt

Don't go breaking my yurt
(Don't go breaking my)
I won't go breaking your yurt
Don't go breaking my yurt
(Don't go breaking my)
I won't go breaking your yurt
Don't go breaking my yurt
(Don't go breaking my)
I won't go breaking your yurt
Don't go breaking my yurt
(Don't go breaking my)
I won't go breaking your yurt
Don't go breaking my yurt
(Don't go breaking my)
I won't go breaking your yurt
Don't go breaking my yurt
(Don't go breaking my)
I won't go breaking your yurt
Don't go breaking my yurt
(Don't go breaking my)
I won't go breaking your yurt
Don't go breaking my yurt.

Port-A-Loo

Inspired by: Waterloo

November 2020

There was a version of this song in "Brexit's a Trick not a Treat?", but lorry queues in Kent and the labelling of Kent on road signs as the "Toilet of England" meant that an update was called for.

"Operation Pisspot" made it into the national press, and featured on "Have I Got News for You?"

My, my, with Port-a-loo
The UK did surrender.
Oh yeah, and we have met our destiny
In quite a similar way.
The Brexit deal Boris has done
Won't have us all on the run.
Port-a-loo - M20 line up, along the way;
Port-a-loo - khazis for drivers on motorway;
Port-a-loo – 'cos of the gridlock, loos are sent;
Port-a-loo - stretching the toilets out over Kent;
Port-a-loo - Finally facing our Port-a-loo.

My, my, we tried to get a deal
But we weren't stronger,
Oh yeah, and now it seems those passports
Are taking us into Kent
And how could we ever refuse

If they lay out so many loos?
Port-a-loo - never mind a deal,
We are not sore.
Port-a-loo - Promise to use them for ever more.
Port-a-loo - Plastic bogs there if you wanted to.
Port-a-loo - Stuck on the road but we still poo.
Port-a-loo - Finally facing our Port-a-loo.

The Brexit game that we can't lose
If they lay out so many loos.
Port-a-loo - Couldn't escape if we wanted to.
Port-a-loo - Brexit is taking us into you.
Port-a-loo - Finally facing our Port-a-loo.

Port-a-loo - Brexit is taking us into you

Port-a-loo - Finally facing our Port-a-loo.

PM rejects his own Oven Ready Deal

Negotiation seemed to be sluggish;
Now Boris and Dom have gone thuggish.
It seems clear that they feel
They signed up to a Deal
Which they have now determined is rubbish.

Britannia Waives the Rules.

Inspired by: Rule Britannia

There was discussion about what version of Rule Britannia to sing on the Last Night of the Proms.

Lyrics refined with Zena Wigram, who sings this on the CD, with orchestration by Roger Knight.

The Government had announced its intention to table a Bill that would break international law in "limited and specific" ways.

10 September 2020

When Boris fi-i-irst, and quite unplanned,
Aro-o-o-ose from out the Te-e-e-elegraph,
Arose, arose, arose from out the Te-elegraph,
Sought to be leader,
The leader of the land,
And wanted Bre-e-e-exit for a laugh.
Rule Britannia!
Britannia waives the rules.
Britain, sadly we acknowledge led by fools.

When Boris we-e-e-ent to Brussels to "get it done",
Propo-o-o-o-o-o-osed his oven-oven-ready Deal
The 'he's got Brexit done' oh yes his Oven-Ready Deal
He hadn't read it,
As reading is no fun
So he didn't need agreement to be real.
Rule Britannia!
Britannia waives the rules.
Britain, sadly we acknowledge led by fools.

.

Inspired by: Rule Britannia

Pacta Sunt Servanda

by Hilary Cashman

*Inspired by "**Good** King Wenceslas"*

September 2020

Down the corridors of power
Helplessly they wander.
MPs face the evil hour -
Pacta sunt servanda.
Tories quail before the jeers
Must they really pander
To the rabid Brexiteers? -
Pacta sunt servanda..

Lies, bad faith and politics
Tear us all asunder.
Let's expose Dom Cunnings' tricks
Pacta sunt servanda.
Boris, sauce that's for the goose
Should be for the gander -
Keep your word ! (oh, what's the use...?)
Pacta sunt servanda.

From Britannica.com:

The Latin formula pacta sunt servanda ("agreements must be kept") is arguably the oldest principle of international law. Without such a rule, no international agreement would be binding or enforceable. Pacta sunt servanda is directly referred to in many international agreements governing treaties, including the Vienna Convention.

Naughty Boy

He is an inveterate liar;
He's made us a global pariah;
As attitudes harden,
Says #IDontBegPardon
A naughty boy, not the Messiah.

Another Distraction

If you seem in a bit of a fix
As UK and EU law don't mix
You can see the attraction
Of sudden distraction,
Promoting the new Joy of Six.

Lockdown Shakespeare

Shakespeare's plays would have turned out differently if they were set in Lockdown conditions. Let us illustrate.

Taming Of The Shrew

ACT 1. A room in Katherine's house and a room in Petruchio's house

Enter KATHERINE and PETRUCHIO to their respective rooms

Alarums and errors

KATHERINE

Why Sir, I trust I may have leave to speak,
Even to the utmost, though I need a leak.

PETRUCHIO

Her lips doth move, her hand raise in salute
And yet there's naught I hear - she is on mute.
Curtain

The Tempest

ACT 1. On a ship at sea, whereat GONZALO and MARINERS, and at the shore, whereat PROSPERO and MIRANDA

GONZALO

While wills above be done, let death be dry.
What is that land which from our ship is seen?

PROSPERO (to Miranda)

The waters wild I made, and you know why;
If they land here, they're stuck in quarantine.
Curtain

Othello

ACT 1. In OTHELLO'S Chamber.

Enter OTHELLO, apparently alone.

OTHELLO

There's none allowed in here, of that I'm certain.
And so I plunge my knife right through the curtain
To check we're clear – oh, see, my dagger slid
And sliced through cloth and this chap who was hid.
Curtain (another one)

King Lear

ACT 1. In the offices of GONERIL, REGAN and CORDELIA

GONERIL

Which one of us can call? You know the rule.

REGAN

There's only one allowed with that old fool.

CORDELIA

One daughter only meets within his bubble?

GONERIL

You go then, sis, for us, he's too much trouble.

Curtain

Twelfth Night

ACT 1. At the Court of Count ORSINO
Enter ORSINO and MALVOLIO

ORSINO

If music be the food of love, play on
Give me excess of it, that surfeiting
The Spotify may sicken and so die;
We'll have the Daily Briefing by and by.

MALVOLIO

We'll hear those vile statistics; nothing more.
And yet they plan to send more shock and awe.
The news we have today's already shocking;
I think I'd better wear my yellow stocking.
Curtain

Much Ado About Nothing

I clicked the mouse and hoped to have a greeting.
Has organiser failed to launch the meeting?
Curtain.

Henry V

ACT 1 . An ANTECHAMBER in the KING's PALACE

Enter KING HENRY and attendants
ARCHBISHOP OF CENTERBURTY is on zoom.

KING HENRY

Prepare the boats and make our way to France!

ARCHBISHOP OF CANTERBURY

The ports are locked – you haven't got a chance.

KING HENRY

Once more to the box sets, dear friends, once more.
What can we do at home within the law?
Curtain

Hamlet

ACT 1. The quayside

Enter POLONIUS and LAERTES. HAMLET is hid.

POLONIUS

Give thy thoughts no tongue,
Nor any quickly furloughed one the work.
Be thou attentive, but by all means distanced.
The friends thou hast, if they have zoom installed,
Save thou their contacts so you'll call at will,
But do not dull thy wall with entertainment
Of each new-made, unchecked, Face Friend. Beware
Of entrance to a tweet-storm, but, being in
Share it, that the opposed may beware of thee.
For every one you follow, read their tweet;
Note each one's rantings, but hold back your post.
Dress well above the waist, for that is seen;
But trousers matter not – they're out of sight.
Neither a borrower nor a lender be,
As Lockdown day's good credit's lost that night.
This above all – your profile should be true,
So they will follow, and subscribe to you

HAMLET

He writeth to Laertes, not to me;
Forgot he that I was still in cc.

Curtain

Romeo And Juliet

ACT 1. At Juliet's balcony

Enter JULIET to the balcony, with smartphone.

Enter MERCUTIO to the street below checking statistics.

MERCUTIO

Broad is the band

JULIET

Through which our words may flow.
I'm waiting here, wherefore art Romeo?

ROMEO

Provided I my details all to Zoom;
Becalmed am I within the Waiting Room.

JULIET *(admits ROMEO)*

Ah your sweet face! I never see your trousers.

ROMEO

The network fails!

MERCUTIO

And plague's hit both your houses'

ZOOM

`Before you go, we trust that you will rate us.`

JULIET

The call hath died, be that its only status.

ROMEO

And frankly I'm more worried at our fate as
Our hospital's run out of ventilators.

Curtain

Act 5: Congestion, Reflection, and Reward of the Undeserving

Virus Cometh

Inspired by: The Gas Man Cometh

August 2020

In January twenty-twenty
The virus came to call
We went for herd immunity,
It didn't work at all.
Johnson tried the nearest phone box
He still came out like Clark Kent
We thought he told us not to work,
That wasn't what he meant.

Oh, it all stops work for the working people too

In April twenty-twenty,
When no one went to work.
And some got furlough money,
Don't consider it a perk.
They said please use the furlough,
So that you don't fire us.
But just exactly how d'you mean,
We should control the virus?

Oh, it all stops work for the working people too

We heard May twenty-twenty,
Mister "Must Take Back Control"
Toured North-East England,
Scored spectacular own-goal.
But if this means that restrictions
Need some easement - please discuss.
The matter is not relevant;
"Rules are for them, not us"

Oh, it all stops work for the working people too

It's June of twenty-twenty
It's time to open schools
And while we are about it
Next month we'll ease the rules
Go to work and to the pub
Remember furloughs will be cut
The Premiership plays football
But the theatres stay shut

Oh, it all stops work for the working people too

It's August twenty-twenty,
They to easing call a halt.
We're not completely sure why,
Except that it's our fault.
I guess that picking clowns to rule
May well produce a farce
So we'll go back into Lockdown,
As he's talking through his "R"s.

Oh, it all stops work for the working people too

And through the long hot summer
They all do no work at all
So it's Autumn twenty-twenty
When the virus comes to call.

Prime Minister's School Report

August 2020

ORAL: Dreadful. Never manages to answer the question
MATHS: Very weak, Thinks 6 is 40. Refers to Fermat's Last theorem, doesn't understand it.
READING: Poor. Struggles to get past the first page of any document.
ENGLISH? Maybe – or possibly Russian, judging by the company he keeps.
WRITTEN WORK: Has largely given this up. When he took part, full of inaccuracies.
POETRY: Cannot manage more than 3 lines. The work does not scan or make sense.
FICTION: Spends a lot of time on this, but fails to develop a realistic plotline.
PLANNING: Fails. Very rarely done, & only at the last minute. European work very weak.
REVISION: Frequently revises "plans", largely because they didn't exist in the first place.
GAMES: Enjoys Hide and Seek, but too inclined to rely on the fridge.
HISTORY: Prefers not to mention his own.
GEOGRAPHY: Rates himself because he went to distant parts of Scotland once. Deluded.
MORAL EDUCATION: Does not understand the basics.
SCIENCE: Doesn't know how to follow this.
ECONOMICS: Economical with the truth.

PREDICTED GRADE: FAIL
(After Mutant Algorithm: Prime Minister).

Explaining the Algorithm - The Three Classes

August 2020

With thanks to John Cleese and the two Ronnies.

UPPER: I am upper-class. I go to an independent fee-paying school.

MIDDLE: I am middle-class. I go to a well-equipped state school.

LOWER: I am working class and live in a socially deprived area.

UPPER: Let me explain the algorithm to you. My grades have been boosted. I've got my place at Cambridge. This seems very satisfactory.

MIDDLE: One of my grades has been reduced. I might challenge this with the evidence of my teacher-predicted grade.

I might get my place.

LOWER: All my results have been downgraded and I have now failed two exams, despite my teacher predicting better grades for me.

I've lost my place.

UPPER: After my time at Cambridge, I might go into Government. I expect to make a lot of money on the side. What wizard wheezes we will be able to cook up after Brexit.

MIDDLE: I hope to get a job in the Civil Service, doing what Upper tells me.

LOWER: I've got no place.

Shoot Now for the Moon

Inspired by "Fly Me to The Moon"

August 2020

£10 billion was to be spent on a mass testing "Moonshot" programme in order to resolve the coronavirus problem before Christmas 2020

Shoot me to the Moon
Let's spaff cash we haven't got
And let me see how much I'll cheat
When talking of Moonshot
And afterwards, big fees planned
And afterwards, it's in hand

Fill my hands with funds,
And let me contract evermore.
Parliament can't see this
As that place is such a bore.
In other words, nothing's true.
In other words, let's Leave EU.

Dido needs a job.
Test and trace is such a mess,
Billions is the budget
Just a hundred, more or less,
False positives, they're not true.
Be positive, Be positive.
we left EU.

Twelve Months of Virus

Inspired by: The Twelve Days of Christmas

This version breaks the rules of the song, but only in limited and specific ways.

10 September 2020

In the first month of virus the PM said to me
"I'm superman I'll save the country".

In the second month of virus the PM said to me
"Another long holiday
I'm superman I'll save the country."

In the third month of virus the PM said to me
"Herd immunity
Another long holiday
I'm superman I'll save the country."

By the third month of virus the PM said to me
"You stay at home
I never said that
Another long holiday
I'm superman I'll save the country."

In the fifth month of virus the PM said to me
"It's not our fault

You control the virus
Don't stay at home
I never said that
Another long holiday
I'm superman I'll save the country."

In the sixth month of virus the PM said to me
"Go back to school
It's not our fault
You control the virus
Don't stay at home
I never said that
Another long holiday
I'm superman I'll save the country."

In the seventh month of virus the PM said to me
"Open the pubs
Don't query contracts
Go back to school
It's not our fault
You control the virus
Don't stay at home
I never said that
Another long holiday
I'm superman I'll save the country."

In the eighth month of virus the PM said to me
"Don't break my yurt
Apps don't really matter
Top grades for rich folk
Scrap Public Health
Open the pubs
Don't query contracts
Go back to school
It's not our fault
You control the virus
Don't stay at home
I never said that
Another long holiday
I'm superman I'll save the country."

In the ninth month of virus the PM said to me
"I'll try a moonshot
Rules are for others
Don't break my yurt
Apps don't really matter
Top grades for rich folk
Scrap Public Health
Open the pubs
Don't query contracts
Go back to school
It's not our fault

You control the virus
Don't stay at home
I never said that
Another long holiday
I'm superman I'll save the country."

In the 10th month of virus the PM said to me
"Sack more civil servants
I'll try a moonshot
Rules are for others
Don't break my yurt
Apps don't really matter
Top grades for rich folk
Scrap Public Health
Open the pubs
Don't query contracts
Go back to school
It's not our fault
You control the virus
Don't stay at home
I never said that
Another long holiday
I'm superman I'll save the country."

In 11th month of virus the PM said to me
"No public protest

Sack more civil servants
I'll try a moonshot
Rules are for others
Don't break my yurt
Apps don't really matter
Top grades for rich folk
Scrap Public Health
Open the pubs
Don't query contracts
Go back to school
It's not our fault
You control the virus
Don't stay at home
I never said that
Another long holiday
I'm superman I'll save the country."

In the 12th month of virus the PM said to me
"Let's start again,
No more elections
Billions to cronies,
Parliament suspended,
Gunboats in the channel,
It's Brussels fault,
Courts lose their powers,
Activist internment,

BBC is over,
Arise Sir Tony Abbott,
No public protest
Sack more civil servants
I’ll try a moonshot
Rules are for others
Don’t break my yurt
Apps don’t really matter
Top grades for rich folk
Scrap Public Health
Open the pubs
Don’t query contracts
Go back to school
It’s not our fault
You control the virus
Don’t stay at home
I never said that
Another long holiday
I’m superman I’ll save the country.”

By the time they get to Phoenix

Thursday 5th November

Inspired of course by: "By the time I get to Phoenix"

By the time they get to Phoenix, and still counting,
He'll see the votes they open, more and more.
He'll rant when he reads the part that says he's leaving
Though he should have left so many times before.

By the time they count Nevada, he'll be raging;
He'll probably watch Fox news and tweet to all,
But the tweets will all be marked as most deceiving,
Off the wall, that's all.

By the time of Pennsylvania, he'll be losing,
As scope widens and Joe Biden's lead is strong,
And he'll cry just to think he's really leaving,
Though time and time they've tried to tell him so,
He just didn't know that he would really go.

The 12 days of Christmas in Lockdown

Inspired by: The Twelve Days of Christmas
At this point gatherings from different households were limited to 6 people.

On the 12th day of Christmas my true love sent to me
6 drummers drumming - *and after they had gone*
6 pipers piping - *and after they had gone*
6 lords a-leaping - *and after they had gone*
6 ladies dancing - *and after they had gone*
6 maids a-milking - *and then*
7 swans a-swimming *(agricultural exemptions now apply)*
6 geese a-laying
5 gold rings *which I immediately pawned because life is tough for the self-employed*
4 calling birds
3 French hens
2 turtle doves, and
A partridge in a pear tree., which is ok - we didn't really need a turkey this year since no-one is visiting.
(Idea by "the Now Show")

The Seven Ages of Johnson

Inspired by*: "All the World's a Stage"*

For him the world's a stage,
And every man and woman just a token;
They have their exits and their entrances;
It matters not how many may be broken.

His acts being seven ages. Let's start at Eton,
Wrecking the play ad-libbing what not learned,
And then the lazy writer, with his pieces
Of scribb'ling whining base, payment not earned
As creepingly he lied. And then the Mayor,
Hanging by knackers, with his two-fold flags
Over his governed city, as when he claimed
Water-cannons, buses, bridges, in the bag.

Then to MP, a Tory for his pains.
He joined and seemed as loyal to the herds,
And yet his lies more lucrative in print,
The pay not matching riches for his words.

Then to decide – a toss-up which was best,
A great defeat as Leaving Lead he planned.
And so he played his part, but sadly won.
The flames of Brexit now were all-ways fanned.

Then as the Sec., of Foreign parts aware.
For best Secs, check your briefs, for what you missed.
But times he rose up badly unprepared;
Zagari-Ratcliffe sits at head of list.

Last scene of all – that ends the British age
Of sense, integrity and due respect,
Is PM's childishness – is he oblivious?
By No-Deal Brexit, Covid bug we're wrecked.

The Leadership We Need?

Inspired by: *Windmills of Your Mind.*

1. Round
Like a wangle with a tangle,
Like a contract with no ships,
Like the Bermuda triangle,
Is he lying ? Watch his lips;
If you see that they are moving
With unlikely "hows" and "why"s,
If it's clear that we are losing ,
While our leaders tell us lies.
Like the contracts cutting corners,
Where the market doesn't bid.,
And so many go to Warners,
But criteria all hid.
interest conflicts? More mind-numbings
Was this all dreamt up by Cummings?

2. When fair dealing's been discarded,
And the snouts are in the trough,
Evidence is disregarded,
And controls have been turned off.
When those helped him win elections ,
Write their code that's full of holes.
When the leader's close connections,
Had him dancing round the poles.
Like the members that are walking,

Up and down on College Green.
Like Rees-Mogg just keeps on talking,
So MPs cannot be seen.
When democracy is dying.
And the relatives are crying.

3. Like a vote with Russian masters,
And a very few rich folk,
Who will profit from disasters,
In the fire-sale when we're broke.
Twenty-nine per cent they voted,
"Let's have Brexit! What the heck!"
But excuse me, had they noted
Tories planned the talks to wreck ?
Boris signed up the agreement,
Didn't know the Irish Sea;
Now the country's in bereavement,
Their "plan" makes no sense to me.
If you don't accept their fogging
You are suddenly aware,
(if you look at what I'm blogging)
That the outcome isn't fair.

4. Like a heel who's not a healer
That you know you cannot trust
Like a Deal without a Dealer
That's designed to make us bust

As you worry at down-dumbings
From the brother's Chum of Cummings
And at Dominic's shortcomings.

ALTERNATIVE ENDING

3. Like an expert chess grandmaster.
Who has every move well-planned .
Like a man whose brain moves faster.
Like a leader of the land.
Like an honest man who's open.
And whose private life is clean.
Like he's now got us all hoping.
Like his mind is sharp and keen.
Like his values and his bearing,
Mean his backing can enlarge.
Like the leadership he's sharing,
Show he's ready to take charge.
Like he's in control, he's calmer,
Like he's conscious of the goal.
Like his life's prepared Keir Starmer
To take on this leading role.
4. Hancock's got some tests he'll mail yer,
If you want, have three or four,
Such deceit has led to failure,
And we can't take any more.
When will Tory toffs concede?
And when can we do the deed?

Get the leadership we need,

Kent Convoy

October 2020

Inspired by: Convoy
Dedicated to those people of Kent and truckers who did nothing to deserve this.

Ok Stander one-nine, this here's the Cluster Duck.
You got a copy on me, Parked-Up, c'mon.
Ah, yeah, 10-4, Parked-Up, fer shure, fer shure.
By golly, it's jam packed from Ashford, c'mon.
Yeah, that's a big 10-4 there, Parked-Up.
Yeah, we definitely got the Big Jam, good buddy.
Mercy sakes alive, looks like we got us a convoy.

Was a heck of a plan for the first day of Jan,
Glad the trailers got some beds.
Cab-over Carl with a permit on.
And a Jimmy haulin' Meds.
Should be headin' for space on M – two - oh.
'Bout a mile outta Ashford Town.
I says, "Parked Up, this here's the Cluster Duck.
"And I'd love to put the hammer down"

'Cause we got a little ol' convoy,
Stuck here through the night.
Yeah, we got a little ol' convoy,
Ain't this a load of shite?
You've all joined our convoy,

You're all gonna get in our way,
We wanta roll this truckin' convoy,
Stuck since yesterday.

Convoy! (Ah, breaker, Parked Up, this here's the Duck)
And, you wanna back off them Meds?
Convoy!
Yeah, 10-4, fifty mile or so.
Ten, roger. Them Meds is hitting their dates up here.
By the time we saw the sun go down
We had ninety-five trucks in all
Makes a roadblock up on the overpass
And customs was wall-to-wall
Yeah, them Tories is thick as tyres on a truck
They even had a Gove on the road
I says, "Callin' all trucks, this here's the Duck
"I'm still in a stationary mode.

'Cause we got a little ol' convoy
Stuck here through the night.
Yeah, we got a little ol' convoy
Ain't this a load of shite?
You've all joined our convoy
You're all gonna get in our way.
We wanta roll this truckin' convoy
Stuck since yesterday.

Convoy! (Ah, you wanna give me a 10-9 on that, Parked Up?)
Convoy! (Negatory, Parked Up, we're all so late
Yeah, them Meds is startin' to missin' their date
Mercy sakes, are you ready for another long wait?

Well we saw 5 lanes all pointin' South
Full o' trucks like trains on rails
Left just one lane for us goin' North
And our trucks all nose to tails
We done the channel, oh mister Raab
Them Customs looked with pity
And now we should be swallowin' road
And headed for the City
There's cars and trucks and coaches too
And a trailer's got Noah's Ark
I think the trucks streamed to that road
When released from lorry park

Well we're still stood still , so let's go for broke
Share a coffee on the verge
But I wonder who can see a Port-a-Loo
Since I've now got an urgent urge.

Ah, Cluster Duck to Kentbuster, come over
Yeah, 10-4, Kentbuster?
Listen, you wanna tell Customs the meds going off, is any way he can get through
Yeah I'm hauling quiche, and I think each of them is going off too

Well we laid to sleep in our cabins all
Prepared to stay all night
I could see we'd got no moving call
But you can wake me if moves in sight
I says, "Parked Up, this here's the Cluster Duck"
"We just livin' through a large own goal
Well I don't feel alive under fifty-five"
" And That's take back control? 10-4"

'Cause we got a little ol' convoy
Stuck here through the night
Yeah, we got a little ol' convoy
Ain't this a load of shite?
You've all joined our convoy
You're all gonna get in our way
We wanta roll this truckin' convoy
'fore the end of day

Convoy! (Ah, 10-4, Parked Up, what's your twenty?)
Convoy! (ROCHESTER? Well, they oughta know what to do with them Meds out there fer sure)
Convoy! (Well, mercy sakes, good buddy, we gonna back on outta here, so keep the bugs off your Meds and the beds)
Convoy! (Off your tail, We'll catch you on the flip-flop.
This here's the Cluster Duck on the side)
Convoy!

(We're stuck, 'bye, 'bye)

Lords of Delight

Inspired by: Transport of Delight

August 2020

Some people like democracy,
Elect their own MPs.
Don't like too much bureaucracy;
They want no hint of sleaze.
Instead of such contortions,
We'll push our friends in hoards.
Appointers and approvers of
The London House of Lords.

Vote very nice please, ching ching
Vote very nice please, ching ching

When you have lost your morals,
But you have cash in hoards,
You'll hear my voice a calling
"Who wants to join the Lords?"
And very soon, with ermine cloak,
You'll tread those famous boards.
In a London Parliament, unelected,
Seven hundred member House of Lords.

Along that train of gravy,
Please line up for a gong.

Just pay up for the Tories;
It shouldn't take too long.
We like to show we're loyal;
We check the noticeboards.
That massive building, generous paying,
London Parliament, unelected,
Seven hundred member House of Lords

We have not any way to go that's fair.
Don't say fair! Where's our share? Don't say fair!

We have not any way to go that's fair.
Don't say fair! Where's our share?
Don't say fair! Bungs to spare!

If no qualifications.
You still are qualified.
Just turn up or don't bother,
But still enjoy the ride.
Three hundred for appearance,
Expenses and awards.
Join with a terrorist l,ady
Son of ex-member, KGB,
That massive building, generous paying,
London Parliament, unelected,
Seven hundred member House of Lords

If you're the PM's brother,
Get there before your Dad.
You won't sit with your sister,
As Boris thinks she's bad.
Now there are some exceptions;
Lord Michael Cashman's one.
But there are few rejections ;
Elections are not done.
If lordships cost a gig or two,
Think what you'll go towards.
It's worth it just to be a peer,
Before the Speaker you'll appear,
Join with a terrorist lady,
Son of ex-member, KGB,
That massive building, generous paying,
London Parliament, unelected,
Seven hundred member,
Seven hundred member House of Lords.
Vote very nice please!

The Archers Comment

Inspired by: Barwick Green (the Archers theme tune)
July 2020

Round and round the case we go,
Thinking who we'll blame next.
Hey let’s try care homes you know,
Though they may all be vexed,
Say procedures
Were not followed there,
Didn’t know what to do.
Though we really
Caused the problem;
Didn’t have a clue.

And now the question who fits up
For Brexit which has gone tits up;
Well since we’re all complainers
Let us blame Remainers.
Well yes they warned us not to Leave;
Their warnings we did not believe;
Fingers in your ear,
Project Fear.

It’s such a shame
If none to blame
For everything PM has done.
As he rambles

Omni shambles
For every single excess death,
And their procurement,
Save your breath.

Yes we discharged without tests.
We do not deserve to be here,
But will fulfil Project Fear.
Every day see Cummings lurk,
And his mates will get the work.
There's PPE and apps to do,
Contracts let to Lord knows who.

Let's keep quiet
About the stats.
Let's hope that no one
Does the maths.
And spin another fable.
Don't talk of league table.
Just obeying orders.
Let's not talk of borders.
For ev'ry one we are talking to,
We pissed 'em.
Mistakes, list'em.
Got no system.
Targets? missed 'em.
Irish Sea?

A mess you'd never believe....

Customs docs are all in a mess.
No-one with sense has said yes.
It's a shambles, let's confess.
Farmers will be sending less.
Consultation? Still we'll wait
Preparations made too late.

Trade and systems buggered up
As far as you can see.
Ambridge farmers are not pleased,
Since they're not on track now.
Hey will MPs find a wheeze;
Please can we go back now?

Perhaps in Parliament,
There's an argument
They know what to do?
Though they really
Caused the problem;
Didn't have a clue.
Oh no we've just
Seen that we're bust.
Who'll Help Us Now?

Inquiry Nightmare

Inspired by Nightmare Song, Iolanthe

August 2020

When I'm lying awake with a dismal headache and
Whether I'll sleep there's no knowing,
Concerned by a cough and the duvet slips off and
I'm worried the way the world's going.
The waiting's inFINite, I hope in a minute
To drop into deep restful slumber;
But the night is half gone, put the radio on
With sleep timer on some hopeful number.
It plays the world news and then I hear whose
Infections spread terrible warning.
It all is depressing, and leaves me still guessing
If sleep's ever coming till morning.
And my mind is all fiery, on Public Inquiry
At least it implies that they're trying
Has the tide really turned, will the lessons be learned?
Or will it be so much more lying?

Well, I get some repose in the form of a dose
With rough throat and head ever aching,
But my slumbering teems with such horrible dreams
That I'd very much better be waking;
From I dream twenty twenty, delays are a plenty
How to Inquire, what's the preference?
Just how should we drive it, as public or private?

Deciding their own Terms of Reference.
And Parliament will pass Inquiries Bill
Which they say is for acceleration
So, the Government choose any chairperson who's
Put in charge of the investigation.
For speed then of course it can all be outsourced
By the way it's twenty twenty-one
I can't quite remember; it may be December
And still no Inquiry's done
So it's now twenty-two, and procurement is due
Establishing who'll be the witness
And who is equipped, no 10 is tight-lipped
About the new Chairman's full fitness
But now are we failing, they're pushing Chris Grayling
But protests prevent that bestowment.
PM's friend from the Garrick, though somewhat barbaric
Is given the job for the moment

Well we've reached twenty three, and a new company
Which is called Faculty Undertaking
Did you see this coming, it's Dominic Cummings
Gets contract, I wish I was waking.
But is that official, Review now Judicial
Questions Short Cummings of Deal
But this isn't backed, Judicial new Act
From last year rules out any appeal

And it's now twenty four, with Election once more,
And so we can't have any cheating
So please no more moaning, it's short-term postponing,
And next year, Inquiry - world-beating.
So we reach twenty-five and, for those still alive,
At last we'll say "On with the show"
But now old Lord Johnson, he tweets from Wisconsin,
"It all seems a long time ago."
"Through evidence wading, with memories fading,
It seems like a mountain you're climbing
Though it's in your diary, this Public Inquiry,
It doesn't seem very good timing"."

Twenty-six, Twenty-eight, getting terribly late
The Government's clear, we have nothing to fear,
Next election brings halt, but it's all been our fault,
The inquiry's been spurned, and what have we learned?
I can clearly see this, that they're taking the piss;
No sensible folk would put up with this joke
I've a headache intense,
and a general sense
Democracy's had its hangover.
But the darkness has passed, and it's daylight at last
And the night has been long, ditto, ditto my song,
And thank goodness they're both of them over!

Reasons for Not Going to Work

As Lockdown 2 came to an end it might be necessary once again to explain absence from the workplace. Fortunately, I had prepared a comprehensive selection of reasons, and it seemed appropriate to add to a book of non-apologies with these apologies.

(I first started these some years ago after receiving a version of the "Bogs have blown" excuse at much greater length from a team-member on the project that I was leading, and I felt it could have been shortened)

Some of these reasons were published with Sarah Watts' musical "Warm-ups".

Introduction

Think I may
Not work today
Tell you my
Reasons why

Couture & Grooming

Shower bust
Think I must
Not be seen
Till I'm clean

Trouser zip
Has a rip
Cannot sew.
Oops! Bad show

My shoe laces
Ripped in places.
Cannot meet
In bare feet.

Doggie poo
On my shoe
Used a cloth
Won't come off

Busy

Dog is sick
Cannot lick.
Need the vet.
Not here yet.

Bogs have blown
Cannot phone.
Plumber's gone
Like our john.

FBI
Happened by
Want to know
What I owe

Neighbour's maid -
Drugs squad raid.
Had to hide
Her inside.

Fred's au pair -
She is where?
She was my
Alibi.

Called Away

Photo op
Local shop;
Must be seen
With the Queen

They want me
On TV
Got to go
Daytime show.

UN gone
Lebanon
Army coup
Need me too.

Arctic meet
Global heat
CO2
Need my view

Small green men
Here again
Got to go.
UFO.

Distracted

Roaming choir
All caught fire
Flaming gown
Must hose down.

Have you heard
Massive bird
Dead; sad loss
Albatross.

In my bunk
Found a monk
Praying so
Rude to go.

Don Maclean
Called again
Funny song.
Very long.

Rolling Stone
On the phone
Old blagger,
Mick Jagger.

Lost or Stuck

Please don't tease
Lost my keys
In a corner
Of the sauna

Donor card?
Very hard.
Couldn't part
With my heart.

Bumble bee
Just stung me
Very hurt
Ripped my shirt.

Slipped and fell
Down the well.
Very wet.
Not out yet.

In a fix
Weetabix
Just too dry
Want to cry

Way Blocked

Dinosaur
At the door
This one winked;
Not extinct.

Rainstorm makes
Large green snakes
Come today;
Blocked my way.

On the train
Met a plane
On the track
Must go back.

Got to hide
Here inside
Paparazzi
Getting nasty.

I'm not free
Fallen tree.
Get by? How?
Still there now.

Problems At Work

I just heard
Floods occurred -
My desk you
Cannot rescue?

Boys in blue
Came for you.
I will stall them
Till you call them.

You say Rick
Called in sick?
My bug is
Same as his.

Conclusion

Making rhymes
Many times
Getting tough
Had enough
Dodgy head
Still in bed
Deepest sorrow
Back tomorrow.

Act 999: Emergency

Everybody Knows What This Foreboded

Inspired by: hearing Barb Jungr singing "Everybody Knows" in a socially-distanced concert in a pub garden brilliantly organised by Dillie Keane.

Friday 13th November
Everybody knows what this foreboded;
Everybody voted though they knew,
Everybody knows his friends are loaded;
Everybody knows they want more too,
Everybody knows this fight was fixed;
The poor stay poor, the rich more rich;
That's how it goes;
Everybody knows.

Everybody knows life can't be peaceful;
Everybody knows why we lock down.
Everybody knows that he's deceitful;
Everybody knows he's such a clown,
Everybody talking in their bubbles;
Everybody wants an end of troubles.
And a life they chose;
Everybody knows.

Everybody knows he has his weakness.
Everybody knows that he can't say when.
Everybody knows the pain is needless;

And he's buggered up the Deal again.
Everybody knows, they can remember,
All still unknown and it's December -
Deal no-shows,
And everybody knows,

Everybody knows, everybody knows
About our woes
Everybody knows

Everybody knows, everybody knows
That's how it goes;
Everybody knows,

Everybody knows he had no exit;
Everybody knows that stakes are upped.
Everybody knows he messed up Brexit;
Everybody knows that Britain's stuffed.
Everybody knows the state is rotten;
And the promises forgotten;
No highs, all lows.
And everybody knows.

Everybody heard that distant drumming;
Everybody knew we stood to lose.
And everybody knew the Plague was coming
If they listened to the news.

Everybody knows where he has been.
But there's gonna be a rating on the screen
That will disclose
What everybody knows.

Everybody knows that Tory cronies
Get the contracts, what a nerve.
Everybody knows the firms are phony
Getting deals they don't deserve.
Everybody knows it's coming apart;
It's your country, have a heart
Before it blows.
As everybody knows.

Everybody knows, the whole world over
About our woes.
Everybody knows.

Everybody knows, everybody knows;
No highs, all lows;
Everybody knows.

Everybody knows, everybody knows;
Although Dom goes
Everybody knows.

When We Break Up (Oyster Snack)

subtitle: "Got Scotland Done"
inspired by "I would walk 500 miles
When we break up, well I know I'm gonna be
I'm gonna be the man who builds the SNP
When I get out, well I know I'm gonna be
I'm gonna be the man who trashed things with EC.

If I don't plan, well I know I'm gonna be
I'm gonna be the man who won't plan next to you.
And if I mess up, yeah I know I'm gonna be
I'm gonna be the man who's messing next to you

But I would fly 500 miles
And I would fly 500 back
Just to be the man who flies a thousand miles
To grab an oyster snack.

When I'm bluffing, yes I know I'm gonna be
I'm gonna be the man who's bluffing next for you.
And when the millions, comes in for the loans I do
I'll won't pass so many pennies on to you.

When I broadcast (when I broadcast)
Well I know I'm gonna be
I'm gonna be the man who broadcasts worse than you.
Easing lockdown (easing lockdown)
Well I know I'm gonna be

I'll be easing lockdown which I shouldn't do.

But I would fly 500 miles
And I would fly 500 back
Just to be the man who flies a thousand miles
To grab an oyster snack.

Dow da da dow (Dow da da dow)
Dow da da dow (Dow da da dow)
Dow da da dow fiddle a fiddle a fiddle a da
Dow da da dow (Dow da da dow)
Dow da da dow (Dow da da dow)
Dow da da dow fiddle a fiddle a fiddle a da.

When I'm lonely, well I think that we will see
Who'll gonna be the ones who quickly fly here too.
And when they're coming, they'll build up the SNP.
They're going to fly around and blindly insult you.

When they go out (when they go out) well you know they're gonna be
They're going to be within the Baxter's, that's so true.
And when they're talking (when they're talking)
They're going to be the ones who will embarrass you..
They're going to be the ones who will embarrass you.

But I would fly 500 miles
And I would fly 500 back
Just to be the man who flies a thousand miles
To grab an oyster snack.

Dow da da dow (Dow da da dow)
Dow da da dow (Dow da da dow)
Dow da da dow fiddle a fiddle a diddle a da
Dow da da dow (Dow da da dow)
Dow da da dow (Dow da da dow)
Dow da da dow fiddle a fiddle a diddle a da
Dow da da dow (Dow da da dow)
Dow da da dow (Dow da da dow)
Dow da da dow fiddle a fiddle a diddle a da
Dow da da dow (Dow da da dow)
Dow da da dow (Dow da da dow)
Dow da da dow fiddle a fiddle a diddle a da.

But I would fly 500 miles, And I would fly 500 back
Just to be the man who flies a thousand miles
To grab an oyster snack.

Fishy Summary

If you carp on EU
Cod won't help you
Our sole in sorrow;
Pollocks tomorrow.

You picked a fine time to Leave with No Deal

The Prime Minister advocated the advantages of leaving with No Deal
Inspired by: You Picked a Fine Time to Leave Me, Lucille
November 2020

In a referendum
Divisions to end-'em
The promises made were immense
We'd be more wealthy
With funds to stay healthy
The adverts pushed folk off the fence
When people were bitter
Some said "I'm a quitter"
Their votes were not used as it seemed
The manipulations
Escaped stipulations
They didn't receive what they dreamed

Now we're led by the lying
Mistakes causing dying
Honesty is what we lack.
Blunders a plenty
Throughout twenty twenty
But Ministers don't get the Sack.
Whatever the cost
We support David Frost
And Frosty the No-Man's his name
Ignoring the nations

We've seen some evasions
But I think the objective's the same

You picked a fine time to Leave with No Deal
When thousands are dying
And still you are lying
We've all in the mire as
We're stuck with the virus
But this one the damage won't heal
You picked a fine time to Leave with No Deal

Targets, they missed 'em
Ain't got no system
Where was it those noble plans went?
They never say sorry
Just park every lorry
On every location in Kent
Supply chains are creaking
And nobody's speaking
Explaining if they've got a plan.
You cant trust a promise
From leaders dishonest
The shit's heading straight for the fan

Friday 13th November

Happy Christmas with restrictions

We can't see everyone we want just when we want to.

Some improvisation may be necessary with Chrsitmas presents

It became important to keep up to date with changing rules

.

Government Guidance: Get Ready for Brexit

December 2020

Government adverts were full of exhortations to "Get ready for Brexit" although what was to get ready for was still not decided

Not Oven-Ready?

In case the excitement's too heady
I think that we'd better go steady.
The Meal's not been costed
And nothing's de-Frosted;
That's not what I'd call "Oven-ready".

Deal with the Sturgeon

From crisis to crisis we're lurching,
Despite all of businesses urging
That their prominent wish
Is to Deal with the Fish,
Or else they must Deal with the Sturgeon.

Ending in Tears

As the key date for each crisis nears,
Forgive me for airing my fears,
That the outcome for Brexit
Will be, just as Covid,
In fact, that they'll both end in tiers.

Events take a new turn

The Christmas 5-day suspension of restrictions was cancelled at the last minute

Though they generally blame non-compliance,
And to questions display their defiance,
Events take a new turn,
Weeks later, a U-turn -
The result of ignoring the science.

Prime Minister of all UK - reprise

Inspired by: Now he is the Ruler of the Queen's Navy (HMS Pinafore, Gilbert & Sullivan)

31 December 2020

An update – the first 3 verses are as before but we wanted to bring in Christmas Eve etc

When I was a hack, I raised a laugh
With silly pieces for the Telegraph
Of bent bananas – what would get a rise
I wrote those articles though they were lies
(He wrote those articles though they were lies)
I wrote those articles and earned good pay
And now I am Prime Minister of all UK
(He wrote those articles and earned good pay
And now he is Prime Minister of all UK)

As journalist I cut a dash
And they made me the Mayor of the London Bash
I invented buses with a funny quirk
With a bridge and water cannons that didn't work
(With a bridge and water cannons that didn't work).
For the bridge and water cannons folk had to pay
But now I am Prime Minister of all UK
(For the bridge and water cannons folk had to pay
But now he is Prime Minister of all UK),

For the Leave campaign I rode a bus
With a slogan on the side that we won't discuss.

Well, I hoped to lose in a glorious way
But sadly, I won at the end of the day.
(But sadly, he won at the end of the day).
I won that vote, though Theresa May
Was then Prime Minister of all UK
(He won that vote, though Theresa May
Was then Prime Minister of all UK)

I got a majority and now I feel
I can threaten everyone we'll Leave No Deal
But I know some would view that as a failure
So instead I will talk about Australia
(So instead he will talk about Australia)
I talked such drivel 'most every day
You can do that when you're PM of all UK
(I talked such drivel 'most every day
You can do that when you're PM of all UK)

The time that I'd like to talk about Leave
Will be afternoon on Christmas Eve
And so to make true my Christmas wish
We'll argue all night then concede on Fish
(They'll argue all night then concede on Fish).
I'll concede on Fish in the light of day
You can do that when you're PM of the whole UK
(He'll concede on Fish in the light of day
You can do that when you're PM of the whole UK).

Now MPs all whoever you may be,
If you want to rise to the top of the tree,
You can treat the electorate as if they're fools
If you're not constrained by the normal Rules
(He's not constrained by the normal Rules)
So, don't hold me to anything I'll say
'Cos I'm Prime Minister of all UK
(So, don't hold him to anything he'll say
'Cos He's Prime Minister of all UK).

Bad Deal versus No Deal

30 December 2020
As I watch the debate that's unreal
And MPs explain how they feel
Some Tory positions
Just like Opposition's:
They prefer a Bad Deal to No Deal.

Not the Biggest Deal in History

Oh BBC this does seem twister-y
With no understanding of history;
Saying Deal for our Trade
Is the biggest we made
When compared to what's lost? That's a mystery.

So what have you come to, my country?

Inspired by "Where Do You Go To, My Lovely?"

31 December 2020

His speeches are full of confusion,
And marked by an absence of fact.
He seldom makes clear conclusions;
More bluster's how he will react.
Yes he will.
And there's favours for friends and relations,
Like the wives of his favoured MPs,
Even though they've no qualifications;
He isn't much bothered by sleaze, no he's not.

So what have you come to, my country,
Believing each thing that he said?
Tell me the thoughts of each voter.
I want to look inside their head,
Yes, I do.
The basis for leaving was feeble,
With lies on a bus that were seen.
It wasn't the Will of the People.
When that changed, he saw 2016,
Yes he did.

And he's only PM 'cos of Brexit,
An incompetent Cabinet too.
Do you think it's now time for his exit,
Along with the rest of his crew,

Oh yes, and all of them?
The entry condition – obedience,
With full disengagement of brain.
Incompetence flows from expedience.
Their failings are all very plain,
Yes, they are.

So, what have you come to, my country,
Believing each thing that he said?
Can I find out the thoughts of each voter?
Would you like someone truthful instead?
Yes, you would?

For an easy life he was desirous;
Hard work was the last thing in mind.
Ignoring the coronavirus,
But that idle response was declined,
Yes, it was.
His appointments were mostly for phonies.
He tried to stop challenge in Court.
He would allocate jobs to his cronies.
As we see in the Audit Report, NAO.

So, what have you come to, my country,
Believing each thing that he said?
Can I find out the thoughts of each voter?
Would you like someone truthful instead?
Yes, you would??

And he lied that his Deal was in order.
He lied that December's enough.
He lied there's no Irish Sea Border.
He lied with his bluster and bluff,
Ev'ry time.
And his jobs always end with his lying,
His speeches untrue,
Yes they are.
He lied that MPs would control things;
But I know we still bear the scar,
Deep inside, yes, we do.

I see where you've come to, my country
Believing each thing that he said.
What now are the thoughts of each voter?
Would you like someone truthful instead?

Na-na-na-na, na-na-na-na-na-na-na
Na-na-na-na, na-na-na-na-na-na-na

2021- What About The Cuts?

Inspired by 1921 - What About The Boy? - The Who

Do you think twenty-one
Is going to be a good year?
Especially if me'n vaccine
See it in together?

Yes I think twenty-one
Is going to be a good year.
It could be good for me and you
With vaccine forever.

We had new reasons
To be extra optimistic,
As somehow with vaccines
We can brave bad weather,

What about the cuts?
What about the cuts?
What about the cuts?
Who'll get stuff all?

Oh but they need it, do we concede it?
We won't pay nothing to no one,
Ever in our lives, though they deserve it,
But we deferred it all then, and where is the proof?

Oh did you read it, yes they need it,

And we should aid them, shouldn't raid them;
Will you say nothing to no-one,
Still support those who don't tell the Truth?

Do you think twenty-one
Is going to be a good year?
Especially if with vaccine
We're here together?

Do you think twenty-one
Is going to be a good year?
Well can you see those who
Are made poor forever?

They have no reasons
To be extra optimistic,
As even with vaccines
They can't brave bad weather.

What about the cuts?

The Donald Went Down to Georgia

Inspired By: The Devil went down to Georgia.
5 January 2021

The Donald went down to Georgia
He was lookin' for some votes to steal
He was in a bind
'Cause he was way behind
And he was willin' to make a deal.

When he came across this official
Sitting on a vote pile and playin' it straight
And the Donald played all on a telephone call
And said, "Man, I want your State".

"I guess you didn't know it
But I can fiddle things too
And if you'd care to take a dare,
I'll make a deal with you.

Now you'll do a pretty good fiddle, hey
But give the Donald his due
I'll bet a fiddle of gold
Against your soul
Twelve thousand votes from you.".

The man said, "Raffensperger's
My name, and I won't sin
This is worst yet, you're gonna regret

This call will be called in".

Brad Raffensperger you won't try that fiddle hard
'Cause Hell's broke loose in Georgia,
And the Donald deals the cards
And if you win, you'll see
That your true story will be told.
But if you lose, the Donald gets your soul.

The Donald opened up his case
And he said, "I'll start this show."
Bad words flew from his evil lips
As he threatened him, you know.

And he said he'd notify a crime
Put Raffen on the floor
And the band of his supporters
Made threats of civil war.

When the Donald finished
Raffen said, "Well, you've had your say, ol' son
But sit down in that chair right there
And let me show you how it's done."

"Fix on the ballots" run boys, run
The Donald's in the House of the Washington
Tweets full of nonsense, supersized fries
Cotton-pickin' voters spot your lies".

The Donald bowed his head
He should know that he's been beat
And it's time to lose that fiddle
Joe Biden needs his seat.

Raffen said, "Donald, just don't come back
And don't you try again
I done told you once, you son of a bitch
You're the worst that's ever been."

"Fix on the ballots" run boys, run
The Donald's in the House of the Washington
Tweets full of nonsense, supersized fries
Cotton-pickin voters spot your lies".

Justice Done?

He called them – "Besiege Washington"
What evidence did he give? None.
His supporters all buy it
And they start a riot,
"In order to see justice done?"

Forget what's said on Marr (Lock Down, Lock Down)

Inspired by: Look Down (Les Misérables)

4 January 2021

After announcing on the Andrew Marr programme on 3rd January that "schools were safe" and that some primary schools should open, despite a weight of evidence to the contrary , Boris Johnson reversed that decisions on 4th January,

JOHNSON
Lock Down, Lock Down
Forget what's said on Marr.
Lock Down, Lock Down,
It's really gone too far

The variant
It took us by surprise

JOURNALISTS
Lock Down, Lock Down,
Because you closed your eyes.

JOHNSON
It's not my fault!
I couldn't work out when

JOURNALISTS
Lock Down, Lock Down
You're shutting schools again.

JOHNSON
The schools are safe.
They cannot catch the plague.

JOURNALISTS
Lock Down, Lock Down,
We think you’ve very vague.

JOHNSON
With the vaccine, we’ll be seen
As the best.

JOURNALISTS
Lock Down, Lock Down

JOHNSON
With a fair wind we’ll try.

JOURNALISTS
How long, we ask
How many more will die?

JOHNSON
Lock Down, Lock Down,
But see my tousled hair
Lock Down, Lock Down,

JOURNALISTS
But are you being fair?

JOHNSON
Now approval for vaccine's done
It's time to start
And our rollout's begun.
You know what that means?

JOURNALISTS
Will it mean we're free?

JOHNSON
No!
It means we get
The vaccine rollout start
You need your shot.

JOURNALISTS
We think we will need two

JOHNSON
We'll get to that.

JOURNALISTS
When can we end the pain?
Each week you need two million shots
What you achieving?

JOHNSON
We'll achieve a lot
Unless there are some problems with vaccine.

JOURNALISTS
We know that problems can indeed occur,
Just as we have seen.

JOHNSON
If we have a fair wind,
If there's no problems with the vaccine,
Yes, our vaccine's done.

JOURNALISTS
Meanwhile what is the plan?

JOHNSON
Don't go from the house.
Do not forget the rules!
Do not forget them,
Like that Cummings man.

JOURNALISTS
Lock Down, Lock Down?
Forget what's said on Marr?
Lock Down, Lock Down?
It's really gone too far.

Open Schools For Now

The Prime Minister declared on 3rd and 4th of January that "Schools are Safe" (though he had some doubts about the people in the schools), but the New Variant was clearly very busy Monday lunchtime, because by Monday evening schools were all to be shut.

5 January 2021

On Sunday he said "Open Schools"
Please don't think we take you for fools.
If this gives you some grief
Then we'll cry at the Brief.
Every time that we must change the rules.

Daily Briefing

General purpose daily briefing for 2021.
Inspiration for this came from a post by Gemma Middleton.

Piffle, wiffle, covid and tears,
World-beating Britain I wish.
Brexit, exit, my hopes and fears,
Got to look after the fish.
Phonies, cronies, contracts for homies,
Billions are spaffed up the wall.
Focus your locus, must call a halt,
As it's your fault after all.

Please Write a Review!

We hope you enjoyed this book

Please leave a review online – for example on Amazon or Etsy.*

As a small independent publisher, Viewdelta Press is very dependent on readers who enjoyed our work to spread the word. So, if you enjoyed the book, please say so in order that others can enjoy the books too.

We can keep you informed of our future projects if you email us at info@viewdelta.com
with an email title of "Keep me posted" or words to that effect.

* If posting elsewhere, you can include our hashtags to help us find the review.
#IDontBegPardon
#Covid19Musical

Reference

Index of titles

Index of references to original songs

Do you need a speaker for your event?

The Art of Comic Song Parody

A lively talk on the challenges of comic parody song, illustrated by audience's favourites and/or references to songs from "Brexit's a Treat not a Trick?", "Brexit's a Musical Trick" or the Covid-19 Musical "I Don't Beg pardon" (which might in fact be audience favourites!) Mike discusses some principles of the emotional tone of the parody, as well as exploring the practical task for the parody poet.

Parody Creation – interactive workshop

After a brief exploration of principles, volunteers – or everyone – can help to create their own comic parody song with Mike's guidance, working in small or large groups. The result can be your copyright property when written.

ViewDelta Press and Charity

ViewDelta Press has made the commitment that ViewDelta's net profit from the "Brexit" books will be donated to UK registered charities.
One way in which we do this is to provide author copies of our books free of charge to charities to sell at their events.
If you would like your charity to sell author copies of our books and to retain the full takings from the sale of the books, please get in touch via the website www.viewdelta.com

The Authors

MIKE CASHMAN
Mike Cashman writes serious and satirical items on Brexit and other topics. and his pieces have been widely shared and appreciated.
Previously he worked in teaching, information systems, project and programme management, and international development.
He blogs at viewdelta.blogspot.com
He is married with 4 children and 10 grand-children.
Mike asked the co-authors to describe themselves and below are the results

FRED CASHMAN enjoys time with family, his two Golden Retrievers, and contributing to the maintenance of the Rule of Law.

HILARY CASHMAN is a (retired) prison librarian, who designed the "Time for Kids" programme to help prisoners enjoy reading storybooks with their young children.

PETER CASHMAN is a charity fundraiser who enjoys attempting to make people smile.

PETER COOK is an Author, Business Consultant, Scientist, Musician, Anti-Brexit campaigner, who declares himself to be “Tragically an only twin.” (Google it!)

PAUL SHRIMPTON is an IT geek, a drummer, and in his spare time dabbles as The Silver Fox, protector of democracies.

"Brexit's A Trick Not A Treat?"

If you have enjoyed this book then you may also enjoy "Brexit's A Trick Not A Treat?"
From the original "Brexitian Fantasy" right up to the controversial "Try a Yellow Hammer round the Whole Country", all of Brexit is here (and even a little of Trump). Theresa May hears "Don't Cry for Leave Now Theresa", Rees-Mogg takes you down to his place by the tower, and we can all sing along to "How do you solve a problem like our Brexit?". Boris Johnson reckons "I'll GATT by with a little help from my friends", and the strains of "Brexit Pie" tell us

> "Bye, bye, to our time with EC.
> We are leaving without grieving for the trashed currency.
> Them good old boys climb the leadership tree
> Saying 'Look what it's doing for me
> Look what it's doing for me'."

Mike Cashman worked for an international development charity for six years, and saw first-hand the effects of the damage to sterling from the Brexit events. So he asks:

> "If you hoped for a Brexit that's sweet
> As a cake you can have and can eat,
> Do you now realise
> The extent of the lies,
> And that Brexit's a trick, not a treat?"

The profits from this book will be donated to UK registered charities.

#BrexitsATrickNotATreat

Brexit's A Musical Trick

You may also enjoy "Brexit's A Musical Trick"

The action takes place in an imaginary country which is considering a Brexit from the European Union. Please consider any resemblance between characters in the musical and living rational sentient 21st century politicians to be purely coincidental.

Boris Valboris has lived his life under the injustice of not being Prime Minister, but he considers whether to lie or not in order to bring this situation to an end, and then battles with his long-term Nemesis, Govert.

Not everything runs smoothly however, as Camerine, Theryline and finally Boris Valboris sing their way to their elusive Brexit. Rees-Moggi lures Theryline into the murky world of "Lovely Tax Breaks". Faragier ("Master of the Spiel") with Widdy, and then later the irrepressible street urchin Corboche have their say (or their song), without having very much impact.

Valboris and others consider how much longer they can stand being with Theryline, and "One Day More" at Chequers is the answer. Four blokes with paste buckets remind the other characters what they have said.

Eventually, however, a mute and lifeless Valboris is carried in and placed on the Leader's Throne. He sends the MPs away, and Mr Grievous laments "Empty Houses, Empty Benches". But Valboris and Cunnings comment "Ain't it a laugh" and conclude "Failure Doesn't Matter in the Past" as their attention is momentarily taken by a coronavirus pandemic.

#BrexitsAMusical Trick.

"Brexit's a Musical Trick" CD / USB

During Summer 2020 the Viewdelta singers recorded 24 of the songs (and a poem) from the Musical "Brexit's a Musical Trick", including many famous tunes. This was recorded in a socially distanced manner, one singer at a time, and mixed to produce this unique recording.

On one CD you can enjoy all these songs, sung by Rachel Ashley, John Asher, Leon Berger, Fred Cashman, Georgy Holden, Helga Perry, Zena Wigram and Marston York. Mike Cashman joins in for the poem.

Act 1 (Camerine)
Do or Die?
We Know What We're Voting For
Hasty Referendum
What Have I Done?

Act 2 (Theryline)
At the End of The Day
We Have Need of a Leader
What Have We Here, Oh You Closet Remainer ?
Lovely Tax Breaks
Master of The Spiel
In My Life
A Poll Full of Votes
Labour People
One's Mascot
Leave and Remain – Led By Donkeys
Do You See The People March ?
One Day More at Chequers
On My Own
An agreement running to 585 pages
A Little Vote of Pain

Act 3 (Boris ValBoris)
Bring Him In
Help Us Out
I Dreamed a Dream
Empty Houses, Empty Benches
There was a wise lady who tackled a lie
Who is this Man?
Ain't It A Laugh?
Failure Doesn't Matter in the Past

"I Don't Beg Pardon" CD / USB

On one CD you can enjoy all these songs from a number of artists.
The lyrics for all these songs are in this book except tracks 15-17 which you can find in "Brexit's a Trick not a Treat?"

ACT ONE - PREPARATION
Boris Has Got a Little List ....Leon Berger
Stay in Your House or Flat ......Peter & Abi Cashman, Simon Cragg
Ill with Covid ....Leon Berger & Selwyn Tillett
Interlude A – Lock Down Shakespeare
Mike Cashman, Georgy Holden,
TAMING OF THE SHREW, MUCH ADO ABOUT NOTHING, OTHELLO
ACT TWO - EXPEDITION
The Ballad of Dom & Bojo .....Andrew Bowes
Barnard Castle, Dom's Ditty.....Fred Cashman
I Don't Beg Pardon, I'm Talking ** from the Rose Garden
Mel Moon
Stand By Your Dom ....Mel Moon
Interlude B - Lockdown Shakespeare:
HENRY V, HAMLET

ACT THREE - PREVENTION
Things that Will Astonish You..Leon Berger & Selwyn Tillett
Man Up, Mask Up, Protect Another Life....Thabani Dube
A Song of Idiotic Prejudice ......Leon Berger & Selwyn Tillett
Heroes, Just for One Day ....Mel Moon

ACT FOUR - DISTRACTION

ACT FIVE - CONGESTION, REFLECTION, AND REWARD OF THE UNDESERVING

We're All Over the Place Online

Here is how to find our online content.
Our hashtags for all online content are

#BrexitsATrickNotATreat
#BrexitsAMusicalTrick
#IDontBegPardon
#Covid19Musical

web: www.viewdelta.com
talks & events: www.viewdelta.com/events
If you want to contact us (e.g. to request a talk or a writing workshop, or to discuss a possible co-operation), please see the contact options on the website.
If you would like to comment on our published content (paperbacks etc) then we recommend using the Facebook pages.
Facebook:
"Brexit's a Trick not a Treat"
"Brexit's a Musical Trick"
"I Don't Beg Pardon" / "Covid19Musical"

Twitter: MikeCashman1
YouTube Channels:
"I Don't Beg pardon"
"Brexit's a Trick not a Treat"

Blog (serious analysis): www.viewdelta.blogspot.com
This is a separate stream of occasional more serious analysis, not referenced to the satirical songs, though you may detect some themes that run through this blog and some songs
Quora: Mike Cashman

What Others Have Said About Our Parody Songs

'This book is a chance to howl in laughter instead of anger. A laser-like humorous side swipe at the Brexit madness.'
Lord Michael Cashman (no relation), on "Brexit's a Trick, Not a Treat?"

"***The best thing to come out of Brexit*** "
Hugh Grant retweeting the YouTube video of "I am the very model of a prejudiced Etonian"

ValBoris dreams a dream of Brexit
Who'd have thought Brexit would so inspire the musical theatre world? After Brexit: The Musical and Now That's What I Call Brexit, another show is on the way. The author Mike Cashman will include the script in a sequel to his book of satirical verses, "Brexit's a Trick Not a Treat"? "The musical begins with ValBoris," he explains, "who is struggling under a great injustice because all his life he has not been Prime Minister."
Sunday Times, 27 October 2019

Not content with his pioneering work in optics, it appears that Dominic Cummings is also catnip to song writers. Mike Cashman, who wrote a musical about Brexit, has penned Stand by Your Dom and The Ballad of Dom and Bojo. Both are available online, as is Song for Dominic Cummings by Fascinating Aida's Dillie Keane.
Sunday Times, 7 June 2020

Amazon Reviews - "Brexit's A Trick Not A Treat?"

☆☆☆☆☆

Great book for Remainers or Leavers!

This very clever and amusing book is a welcome relief from all the misery of Brexit. Doesn't matter whether you are a Remainer or Leaver - just sing along and enjoy with friends and family!

☆☆☆☆☆

Sing-along with Brexit

If you have no idea what is going on, or want to live the happy days of Brexit chaos in musical form - this book is for you. It contains over 100 pages of adaptations of popular songs with witty lyrics for different stages of the Brexit chaos.

☆☆☆☆☆

Better to laugh than cry

Whatever your views on Brexit, it dominates the news agenda and demands a response. This book is a light-hearted and honest response to the travails of British politics since 2016. It cuts through the nonsense with playful lyrics to recognisable popular tunes. Sing along in your head (or our loud if you're feeling bold!)

Amazon Reviews - "Brexit's A Trick Not A Treat?" (continued)

☆☆☆☆☆

Ideal gift!

Brilliant! A witty and entertaining book, this would make an ideal present for those 'hard to buy' for people. Takes some of the animosity out of the Brexit situation. Well done!

☆☆☆☆☆

You can't argue with the title!

Extremely inventive parody of the highest quality, which succeeds in delivering a serious message on this most significant issue of our times.

☆☆☆☆☆

Has you singing along

A fresh and enjoyable approach to Brexit. Very well written parodies of well-known songs that have you singing along.

☆☆☆☆☆

Superb

Very clever, very funny. A much-needed lighter take on Brexit. Highly recommended.

www.ingramcontent.com/pod-product-compliance
Lightning Source LLC
Chambersburg PA
CBHW051449050726
47593CB00005B/1990
* 9 7 8 1 9 1 6 2 4 8 6 4 9 *